# *Weathering Shame*

by

Kevin Mannix

&

Linda Rota, LSW

# WHAT PEOPLE ARE SAYING ABOUT WEATHERING SHAME

*"I commend both Linda and Kevin for their willingness to share their very intimate stories. With their combined skills and experiences they make a powerful team in the effort to help others overcome the painful experiences that accompany mental illness and substance abuse within the family. I am grateful that they decided to strengthen the Maine Community by sharing their journey with us."*

**Angus King**
**US Senator ME**

*"People are more complex than the simple identities we hold. That's the thing I especially appreciate about Weathering Shame. In it they dig deep to reveal the complexity of the people they are, beyond their labels or public personas. It takes an act of courage for a person to do this introspective work – to take a hard look within where many of our private, shamed experiences reside – let alone to reveal these tender memories and vulnerabilities publicly. But that's exactly what Kevin and Linda do in Weathering Shame."*

**Bob Fowler, LCSW**
**Portland, ME**

*"In our culture, the shame and stigma around these conditions keeps many who suffer from them, not to mention their families, from reaching out for help. You have let these people know that they are not alone and that they can find support. Kevin, thank you for using your local fame to benefit the community. You are someone that others trust, which makes the impact of your story all the more powerful. Linda, thank you for encouraging Kevin to tell his story and sharing your own and for your many years of service as a social worker."*

**Chellie Pingree**
**US Congress, ME**

"*Weathering Shame grants readers, burdened by shame, the permission to say 'I'm hurting, but I need to move forward.' This book empowers readers to move from hopelessness to hopefulness. After more than 30 years in the field of mental health, I am confident there is no medication for hope. Hope requires effort, people must become vulnerable and open themselves to feeling uncomfortable at times, where real healing begins.*

*Weathering Shame could be instrumental in facilitating group therapy such as a book club group in a clinical setting. It takes people of integrity, like Linda and Kevin, sharing their personal and sometime painful experiences of shame and stigma to empower others to seek help and begin their own healing journey. Congratulations on a job well done!*"

**John Rota, Jr. M.S.**
**Rehabilitation Therapy Supervisor II, Retired**
**State of Connecticut**
**Department of Mental Health and Addiction Services**

"*Kevin and Linda's willingness to share their story allows so many others, who are living with mental illness, feel like they too can come out of the shadows. The stigma and fear attached to mental illness is a battle we are still fighting and this book will serve to be another way to help provide education for all as well as hope and support to those on their own personal journey.*"

**Mary Haynes-Rodgers, LCSW**
**Executive Director**
**Shalom House, Inc.**

*Weathering Shame*

Written by Kevin Mannix and Linda Rota, LSW

Published by Bryson Taylor Publishing
ISBN 978-0-9882940-4-2
LOC PCN 2015937405

Cover Photography by: Port City Photography
Graphic Designer: Donna Berger
Edited by: Darrin A. Landry and Lindsey K. Le Gervais, Ph. Dc.
Foreword by: Lindsey K. Le Gervais, Ph. Dc.

BRYSON TAYLOR PUBLISHING
199 NEW COUNTY ROAD
SACO, MAINE 04072
WWW.BRYSONTAYLORPUBLISHING.COM

# DEDICATION

*Kevin*

*This book is dedicated to my late Grandmother Mary Riley
who afforded me times of safety, happiness
and encouragement throughout her life.*

*And to my sons Jeff and Taylor, you are my inspiration
and hope. I am so proud to be your father.
Know that I love you with all my heart.*

*Linda*

*To my mom, Anne Benedetti Rota, who I have missed
every day of my life and I know is my guardian angel.*

*To my stepmom and dad, Carol and John Rota.
Thank you for your love and guidance
throughout my life.*

*And to my two beautiful daughters,
Annah and Emily, who have taught
me the meaning of unconditional love,
true happiness and joy.*

# TABLE OF CONTENTS

| CHAPTER | TITLE | PAGE |
|---|---|---|

# PREFACE

Kevin and I have known each other for twenty years. We were neighbors, married to other people, on a delightful little street in Portland, Maine. We both moved away from the neighborhood and eventually lost touch. I ran into him in 2009 at a high school football game and a short time after that we began dating. While we were dating, we talked in depth about his recent healing journey and how after his divorce he decided to start intensive therapy. I listened with admiration, learning about his life and the other side of this man I did not really know beyond neighborly conversation.

He discovered many unresolved childhood traumas and realized it had impacted his life. He was trying to understand how and why he had made the choices in his life and talked about being embarrassed with how he grew up with an alcoholic father and a mentally ill mother. He was working on weaving those experiences into his life and becoming aware of how they have impacted his entire life. It was surprising, as I never knew this part of Kevin, yet it sounded so familiar to my story and the work I had done years earlier.

Nearly everywhere Kevin and I went, someone would comment on his weather forecasting and how they enjoyed watching him on the WCSH Morning Report. People would often comment, "you three are like family to us", referring to the then team of Lee Nelson, Sharon Rose Vaznis and Kevin. They would also say that they had to start their day with them.

I asked Kevin a few times if he would ever be willing to share his story of personal healing with his viewers as he is so admired and respected in his field. I kept encouraging him that many people would benefit from hearing that he had gone through some hard times and was working on his personal growth. However, Kevin thought no one would want to hear his story or it would not make a difference, to him or them. He did not believe there were that many people who struggled with stories of shame.

A few years later, an opportunity came up at the station to do something different and Kevin mentioned developing a piece on this subject of shame and stigma.

After much collaboration, *Kevin's Story* was born and aired on WCSH 6 in September 2013. It was fantastically produced and we were so grateful to the staff and management for their support and hard work. The public response was overwhelming, and people in the community kept asking for more on this subject.

Thousands of people expressed gratitude towards this spotlight on shame and stigma. As a result, we were inspired to write this book to promote awareness and a more comprehensive look at how shame and stigma have molded our individual journeys.

Our hope is that our story may help others to embrace their personal experiences in order to live a happier life that is free of any lingering shame and stigma. This book can be used as a model for personal encouragement, support and inspiration. It is not our intention or place to diagnose those who find significant relevance in the experiences we are sharing.

Since Kevin's career as a television weatherman played such a pivotal role in his positive personal development for over 25 years, it was a natural fit to use weather terms that paralleled the feelings we had around shame and stigma. We decided to organize the book so that each chapter used analogies pertaining to weather terms. We gave each chapter its own basic definition, each mirroring the content of that story. The format is a *7 Day Forecast* with each day reflecting a different aspect of weather, or in our case, a different phase in our lives.

In chronological order, each chapter builds on the last. Kevin starts each chapter, talking about the weather term for that chapter. He then writes about his experiences and thoughts around that time in his life, followed by my thoughts and experiences for that chapter. Each chapter is divided into two sections: first Kevin's story, then mine.

Kevin says life is similar to weather: always changing, with many elements to consider, and always a challenge. The unexpected challenges presented with the weather were a very suitable framework when describing the guise of shame and stigma in our lives.

The title, *Weathering Shame*, speaks for itself: shame is hard to overcome and it can weather a person. Our hope with this book is simple: that our stories encourage readers to begin a journey towards reclamation in order to have more sunny skies ahead.

*Linda Rota, LSW*

# FOREWORD

How do we learn particular behaviors, mindsets, and traditions? According to well-known learning psychologist Albert Bandura, we learn through others. We reproduce behaviors and obtain self-beliefs based on the people and experiences in our lives. The people who are significant to us are likely to influence us in ways we may not understand, both positive and negative.

Along the same lines, social psychologists agree that we create self-beliefs in accordance to social stigma, or the societal perceptions of ideologies we may hold dear to ourselves or as a group of people. The world of mental illness is filled with individuals who have learned behaviors based on their experiences, obtained self-beliefs that are reactive to the negative attitudes around them, and resulted in repression of reality.

The authors, Kevin and Linda, write "Weathering Shame" to rise above the stigma that plagues individuals with mental illness, in particular those who suffer great shame and negative self-beliefs that impact the course of their lives. They offer an honest and poignant recollection of how significant people and experiences impacted their lives through a reflective narrative of real, relatable stories. A book on mental illness told through personal stories is particularly rare in the field, but serves as a powerful platform for allowing those coming from a similar locus to relate, reflect, and take action. Kevin and Linda offer a brave telling of how we can travel through mental illness and personal struggle to eventually reclaim our lives and relationships.

It is important to acknowledge that these stories, of overcoming stigma and mental illness, are not intended to be read like a manual to success. Mental models and self-beliefs are formed in exclusive ways in accordance to the individual; therefore reclamation will be different on each journey. Instead, these stories serve as a formidable prototype to reclaiming ones life ---a model of hope. We may choose to read Kevin's story Linda's story or both, but either way, readers will be inspired by the authors' desire to share their journey to reclamation.

*Lindsey K. Le-Gervais, PhDc*

# 1

## CLOUDS BREAKING FOR SUNSHINE

### *The Story Behind the Book*

*Kevin's Story...*

"Good morning, Lee and Sharon, and good morning everyone. It is a beautiful morning outside to start your day and the satellite shows clear skies. As we check temperatures..." Yes, that's me, Kevin Mannix, the chipper morning weather forecaster for over twenty-five years for NEWS CENTER'S Morning Report, the local NBC affiliate, which is seen throughout the states of Maine and New Hampshire. But when the camera goes off, I turn to the computer and another side of me emerges. This is the side of me I will be introducing to you in this book; the one that has been overshadowed by shame, fear and guilt.

Why am I personally putting myself out there for the public to see? I go back to my wife, Linda. She has been a social worker for thirty years and has her own personal shame journey that you will read about throughout the book. She tells me that many people she has worked with have a powerful story but they are often afraid or too full of shame to tell it. People often think they are alone in their struggle, especially around feelings of shame. It is with her encouragement that I am able to tell my story, which she insists will inspire others to share theirs. It took a while for me to believe this and understand that I might influence others by sharing my journey, but I truly hope I can.

My story is deeply personal to me for sure. Growing up as a child of an alcoholic and the stories that diverged from the experiences I had, I believe, relay great sensitivity yet relevance to those who have similar stories. I am sharing my experiences with my demons and how I now choose to deal with them. May my story and journey to reclamation inspire others to share similar stories.

*Kevin's Story* aired on WCSH6, Portland, Maine, in September 2013 on the Morning Report. It was a week-long series tackling the subject of shame and stigma. Linda and I told our personal stories, shared our struggles and how we ultimately reached out for help and the type of help we received.

The series included guest speakers, professionals, and segments of an in-depth interview with Linda and me, and a morning where viewers could call in to the helpline *211*. The response to the series was overwhelming; the website received thousands of hits to view the series and I received hundreds of emails from individuals and agencies thanking us for talking about shame.

This response continues today. We often have people stop us when we are in public and thank us for sharing the stories. We love and encourage that. We have been honored to be recognized by Crossroads with the *Community Leaders Award*, the *CEO Special Recognition Award* from Crisis and Counseling, and the *Hope Award* from Shalom House for bringing light to the dark subject of shame and encouraging people to get help.

We are very thankful the series turned out so meaningful to thousands of people all over the state and beyond. We received feedback from many viewers saying they started counseling and several others said the series literally "saved their lives". This has been especially gratifying to us -to think that we can bring awareness to the public and possibly help someone. WCSH continues to run the Public Service Announcement (PSA) from *Kevin's Story* to encourage people to reach out for help if needed. Some of the segments are still available on their website.

*Kevin's Story* grew out of my wife's passion to address the topic of shame and stigma that both of us have dealt with our entire life. The best way to tell the story behind the series, and now the book, is to have Linda share why she believes in its message so much. She is deeply passionate about this subject. So Linda, take it away.

*Linda's Story:*

*To believe your own thought, to believe that what is true for you in your private heart is true for all men, that is genius.*

Ralph Waldo Emerson

Growing up in beautiful coastal Connecticut was magical. With its incredible beaches and powerful ocean, I always retreated to the waves to soothe my soul. Just like in Maine, the sounds and rhythms of the waves always made me feel better. I would quickly get lost in my thoughts and feelings, especially as a teenager. The one thought that would never escape me was about my mom. I had very little memory. I was only seven when she died, and she had been in and out of my life all of those seven years. Sitting by the waves, I would wonder what she was or would be like as a woman and a mother. Over the years, I had heard that she was very beautiful and lit up any room she entered. My dad fell in love with her instantly. Pictures do show that she was stunning, and I also heard she was very kind and loving.

What I wrestled with was the other side of her, the times her mental illness would take over and she would do crazy, unexplainable things. I heard many stories, and remember some of these incidents that happened. I never really had a clear idea of who my mother was, except that she took her own life when I was seven and I missed her.

Life was very busy for me as a child. I had a great father (still do!) and three wonderful brothers. My stepmom and I had many conflicts at first, yet managed to live together okay and we are much closer today. I was very busy with work, sports, school, chores, friends, neighbors, hobbies and my extended family. I earned great grades, received some nice honors, and felt accomplished in an external way. I had a very structured life and high expectations from my parents. But that did not stop me from often thinking about my biological mother. I wanted to know and hear about her. I wanted to talk about her. My dad did not talk about or mention my mom much. He would occasionally share something and I would soak it up like a sponge. It wasn't that he did not want to tell us more, it was just a hard subject for him. The biggest struggle was within myself; I struggled with what I *did* know. How do I possibly tell people my mom was mentally ill and took her own life?

Friends would ask about my *real* mom and my stomach would sink and to this day is still a trigger for high anxiety. I would try to stay calm on the outside and reply that she was in an accident and was hit by a truck. Not *exactly* the whole truth. I certainly did not feel like telling them that she was mentally ill, contemplated suicide for years, was committed to the state hospital, escaped, and threw herself into the path of a big truck on the highway. Who wants to hear that?

I felt like hiding under a rock whenever the subject of suicide came up in college, and since I studied social work and criminal justice, the subject came up often. I was sure someone would find out about my mother and I would be so embarrassed. Maybe they would pressure me to talk about it, and then what would I say? I always wondered if I would end up ill like her and perhaps contemplate taking my life, maybe at age forty, just like her.

I share this to illuminate how my passion for tackling shame and stigma evolved. I wanted to talk about my mother but did not know how. It is not like she had heart disease or cancer, that would have been much easier to say or maybe more socially acceptable. She was mentally ill. She committed suicide. There is

5

such a stigma to mental illness, and herein lies the problem. If shame and stigma in our society keep us from sharing our truth, then we learn to move around it; we never really embrace it and learn to weave it into our lives. *Our truth gets buried.* The core of who we are and what we experienced gets buried as well. We are disconnected from ourselves in many ways.

Life went on after my mother's suicide. I had many wonderful experiences and adventures in my childhood and as a young adult. I partied and traveled often and have many great memories. However, I must say there was always a piece of me that was unresolved, that there was a disconnect around my childhood and my mother. I felt I had a secret that I did not want to keep but did not know how to let it out.

When I was in my mid twenties, I finally fell apart after a big life event and started counseling. Once I started to talk about my childhood and my mother, sobbing every session, I realized I never knew the impact it still had on me. I was a client of this wonderful counselor for two years, and slowly became whole; connecting all the pieces of myself and feeling better than I ever had. I started to understand myself and why I felt the way I had all my life.

Fast forwarding to today, I am now fifty-five as I write this book. I have worked with thousands of people in the field of social work and have been honored to hear their stories and struggles. One thing has become blatantly clear: I have repeatedly witnessed the theme of shame over and over again. People often start talking about their lives and get stuck, often embarrassed or ashamed to tell a certain part of the story. They sob because of their pain. It always reminded me of how afraid I was to tell my story and the feelings I experienced in my life once I started letting go. I have embraced my life story, feel no shame or stigma around it now, and feel proud of who I am.

This is the motivation behind the book. In order to heal, we need to break down the barriers and talk about hard subjects. We must be okay with all types of illnesses and encourage people to reach out. We must embrace all parts of ourselves and share our stories and when we are ready, we can start to be free.

Why are certain subjects, such as mental illness, so hard to talk about? Why are certain illnesses acceptable and others not and who decides? Can we change this idea so that people can live freely? These are the questions I have asked myself for years and the passion behind this book.

# 2

## THUNDER AND LIGHTNING

### *Our Early Years*

*Thunder is that sharp clap or rumbling sound you hear after a flash of lightning. The intensity and type of sound depends on the distance between you and the lightning discharge...*

*Kevin's Story: the early years...*

I remember a day when I was about ten and my dad took me to Fenway Park. He loved The Red Sox and when he was sober we would watch the game on TV or listen to it on the radio. He would talk about great players he loved when he was growing up and he taught me the rules of the game. Dad said the more I knew about the game, the more I would enjoy the sport. It was one of just a few things I remember we could talk about. That is why going to Fenway for the first time and seeing a game in person was a big deal and fond memory for me.

It was a sunny, warm Sunday and the Sox were playing a double-header. Not a split day-night affair, one being a make-up of a recent rain out. Oh no, it was two full games with a 20-minute break in between for one price.

Back then you could not watch both games on television. TV would broadcast the first game, and game two was only on the radio. You can understand why it was quite a treat to see both games.

I remember the Red Sox won the first game and that Dad bought me a Fenway hot dog, still my favorite meal to this day. He never bought me much and this is, unfortunately, one of few good memories of time spent with him.

Halfway through game two, a big thunderstorm forced the rest of the game to be postponed. I remember leaving the park and standing in one of the garage doors on the Landsdown Street side of the ball park while the rain poured down on the pavement. Another memory that sticks out was the frequent lightning and almost constant thunder.

My dad held my hand and said, "God sure is having a busy day in Heaven today rolling out his barrels of garbage." He went on to explain that's what was making all that noise. And the lightning? Well, he told me it was the angels with flashlights that were running low on batteries; they were flicking on and off while trying to keep the road lit for God to see. It sounded good to me. I guess because it was one of the few times I can remember feeling safe with my dad.

More times than not though, my dad was stumbling into the house after I was in bed and slamming the door like those loud claps of thunder at Fenway Park. He would talk loud and curse constantly. My mother would say he talked loud because he was hard of hearing and hardly ever used his hearing aids. Of course that did not explain the stumbling. The truth was that he was drunk. Mom would say he only had a couple of drinks after a long, hard day at work. Now I know she was only trying to protect me from the ugly truth, or maybe she was in such denial of my dad's drinking that she honestly believed what she was saying. Either way the process was very confusing. As a child you see and hear life around you and these observations are very real. Then you are told, repetitively I might add, that it is not what it appears.

One eventually loses confidence in one's ability to trust in one's self, one's feelings or the process to make clear decisions.

In my case, I would wait to see how everyone else felt about something before offering an opinion. Very rarely would a thought or action be a Kevin original. An example of this was on my first day in therapy, when the counselor asked me to write down some things I liked about myself and what I wanted to get out of our sessions together. It took me three or four days to come up with one point. I did not even realize how out of touch I was with myself. It was an utter shock. I still remember my number one, which was to find out why I was unhappy most of the time.

Here is an example of what I refer to as "seeing was not believing" growing up in my house. We moved several times. In fact we moved eight times between grades one through eight, which meant eight different schools. Most moves involved all of us, but a couple of times it was just my mom and I moving to her mother's house. A few times we moved in the middle of the night. Mainly because Dad spent all the rent money on alcohol and they needed to escape because they did not have the money.

The excuses my parents gave me was that we moved because of a mean landlord or no heat in our apartment. However, I know Dad spent all the money on alcohol. This was confirmed one of the times we moved in with Gram, my maternal grandmother. I woke up to a fight in the middle of the night. My grandmother was yelling about my dad's drinking and how he had no money for the rent. I did not hear what he said to her but it must have been pretty bad because she grabbed a frying pan off the counter and hit him on the head with it. He ran out the door and my mom was crying. My father would often leave and not return for days. To this day I still do not really know where he went, where he stayed, or who he stayed with. I remember feeling scared but just went back to bed because it was a typical experience.

When I got up the next morning, I asked my mom what had happened. She laughed and said to me, "oh dear, you must have been dreaming- that did not happen." Gram backed her up at the time, but she did admit to me years later, when I was in my teens, that she did it and was not sorry about it. However, the message was well ingrained in me by then: don't trust anyone but yourself!

In an ironic twist, my grandmother died as a result of being run over by a drunk driver one night. She was living across from a supermarket, and would have to cross the busy Massachusetts Avenue on a regularly basis to shop.

I believe that when I was younger, some adults, especially teachers, stepped in when they could to help me out. I did have some positive influences, although I did not see it then. The environment I grew up in as a child, due to my father, left me feeling I only deserved negative consequences.

As a child I suffered from severe asthma, which I grew out of in high school. An example of the feeling of deserving negative consequences happened in the second grade. I attended a Catholic school in Cambridge, Massachusetts, and had to walk two miles to school every day. One really cold and dry morning I started walking and did not get very far before finding it almost impossible to breathe. I sat for a while until I caught my breath and began walking again, only to get about half way to school before I had to stop again. When I finally got to school I was almost a half hour late. Being late meant raps on the knuckles with a ruler. I told the nun to call my mom and she would confirm that I had asthma. She did but my mom thought 'rules are rules no matter the excuse' so I got punished for being late to school. My dad could have driven me sometimes but he said he could not be late for work. I found out when I was older that he left early to stop by a bar before work. It was not a recipe for making a child feel important.

The knuckle rapping continued four more times until a young nun stepped in and stopped it. She recognized that I was indeed having breathing problems and that I needed help; I was very lucky like that.

I recall living a block away from the Cambridge dump. On hot days, the smell from the dump was horribly nauseating. The city park and recreation sat next to the dump, and even with the stench of the garbage, I wanted to go to the park to play. Mom would not let me go at first, but by late August, she suddenly had a change of heart and sent me over to play. The city recreation director assigned to the park that summer was named Kevin. He was kind and gentle, and we hit it off immediately. Kevin taught me how to play baseball and basketball. You can imagine the fun I had being there with him.

One of the rules was that the children needed to wear sunscreen. A good thing for me because then, and still today, I could burn really fast with my lightly freckled skin. One day my mother forgot to cover the back of my neck with sunscreen. Before long, Kevin noticed I was bright red and he sent me home to be cared for. A few blisters immediately formed and I was in severe pain. When my dad got home, he rushed me to the hospital, where the doctor said I had second degree burns. He lanced the boils and applied medicine on the burns to prevent infection. What I remember most is that it hurt like hell. Later my mother admitted she forgot to put sunscreen on me that day, however she quickly placed the blame on me, saying I could have put my shirt collar up to prevent it. I know most kids wore t-shirts, but my mother had me wearing dress shirts so I would not look like a slob. It seemed like it was always something I did wrong.

When I was fifteen, an older guy that worked at Cambridge Electric, by the Charles River, decided he wanted to get some boys together and fix an old boat up. He had the idea that we could fix the boat up and start the Sea Scouts, similar to the Boy Scouts. The boat needed a lot of work, so a few times a week after school, me and about 9 other boys spent the winter sanding, painting and fixing the boat up. We managed to scrape some money together, and the next summer we headed down the Charles and out to Cape Cod. I was looking forward to it because it was ten days away from my mom and dad. We spent the nights on the boats, and one time even had to follow a ferry's wake to Nantucket in rough waves. I had a blast, and remember feeling sad as I was heading back home.

My mom and dad were waiting at the dock when we arrived. My dad was wearing a pair of slippers and a bathrobe. Driving home was mostly silent, and no one asked if I had a good time or asked for any details of the trip. It was all about how much they missed me and how sad they were the whole time. I could not wait any longer; I had to ask why my dad was dressed for bed in the middle of the day. At first my mother told me that Dad had suffered a heart attack while I was gone and had just been released from the hospital. He was on bed rest, but he needed to drive her to the dock to pick me up because she did not drive. The story I heard was that she had been in a bad accident when she was a "detective", which might not have been true. Perhaps her anxiety, or the multitudes of pills she was on, prevented her from driving. After my continuing interrogation, Mom came clean and told me that Dad had actually been in a detox center. She was irritated and mad, confessing that Dad had been found drunk and sleeping on the side of a busy Boston highway. My father sat quietly, not

14

saying a word. My mother was the talker in the family, and I don't know if it he was just letting her ramble, or if he actually felt genuine shame over the incident. The conversation ended with her pointing out the reason he got drunk was that he was upset that I was growing up too fast and had gone on my first trip away from home. My idea of controlling this in the future was to just stay home, thinking everything would be fine.

I did not go away again until after I graduated high school, and to this day, I get nervous and anxious when I travel. I am convinced that it is a direct result of the circumstances I experienced while growing up.

Another example of my dad's poor communication skills was our father-son talk about sex. In fact, there wasn't much talk, just action. For my sixteenth birthday, Dad took me to a run down strip club and bar. After my dad had a few drinks, he sent me with one of the girls to a really dark and small back room. The girl was probable late 20's or into her 30's- it was hard to tell. I do remember she had long, dark scraggly hair- I thought she practiced voodoo or something. She pretty much took charge, as I was scared and nervous but did not know how to stop it. One of my fears was disappointing my dad, so that was where I had my first sexual experience with a woman. He wanted to take me back for my seventeen birthday, but I found enough courage during that year to say no. But the damage was done. Going forward, I could have casual sex without any problem, but seriously struggled with deeper feelings or intimacy. I had feelings of shame when it came to love and sex for a long time, and I never knew the two were not mutually exclusive. I still feel a bit of a stomach ache writing about the shame I associated with it.

The message of not trusting anyone was brought home again in a major way on my eighteen birthday, when I had just graduated from high school. We lived in Arlington, about ten miles away from Boston, and Dad's gift to me was a trip to South Boston with just the two of us. He told me he had a big surprise he could not wait to give me. Even though it was a short drive, less than thirty minutes, it felt like hours. I was extremely anxious because in the past my Dad's birthday surprises were usually not very good. As you read this, I am sure you will understand my past apprehension and the anxiety surrounding surprises.

We drove up to this lovely two story home and knocked on the door. A woman I had never met answered and was happy to see us, especially my Dad. He kissed her on the cheek, then she shook my hand, leading us into this big living room where another man sat waiting. And then the surprise was revealed. Dad, beaming with joy, announced, "Happy Birthday Kevin. Say hello to your brother Fred Jr." Wow, a real surprise all right! Fred Jr. stood and extended his hand and said, "nice to meet you brother." I shook his hand but said nothing out of sheer shock. I sat down looking at him and realized right away that he was a young version of my father. He looked far more like him then I did, so from that moment on I wondered if I was really his son (an issue we never talked about).

Fred Jr. was older; mid twenties maybe. I did not ask because I do not think I said much or knew what to say. I think I was in shock, mixed with feelings of disappointment followed by sadness and anger. What hurt most was that my father never told me about his other son, and kept this secret from me for so many years. It was this sense of utter betrayal that bothered me. Once, my father mentioned that he was married for a short time before he met my mother. What he never told me was that I had a brother that was conceived from that short marriage. I became numb by all the lies and the deceitful environment that I grew up in, which taught me to build walls and easily discard relation-ships. As time went on, I never wanted to know the truth. As a matter of fact, I don't even want to know now. In my mind, what difference would knowing the truth make?

We left with promises of keeping in touch, although I never saw him again until a family reunion of the Mannix family in Massa-chusetts about five years ago. We talked a bit and laughed about our first meeting, but attempts to stay in touch never seemed to happen. Sadly, I am not sure if he is even still alive. Other than my sister Melissa and two sons, I have no real sense of being con-nected to my family. I feel that more with Linda's family and a couple of close friends that are like brothers to me. I love being around them but sometimes I feel an emptiness and loneliness inside.

As I mentioned before, moving all the time was the norm in my family. My last two years at Arlington High School was the first time I was at a school for more than a year. I had been in ten dif-ferent schools before my junior year of high school, which con-tributed to making me a loner. There was no reason to make friends, only to lose the connection faster than I could develop one. To me it was if they had died without a chance for me to say goodbye; so sad and horribly painful.

The excessive moving was only one part of the problem. The Sun-day visits to my cousin's home stopped suddenly after my mother and her sister got into a family feud, ironically over their husbands' drinking. We never went back as a family to visit them again. That's how it worked in my family- I could never talk to them, or I would be in trouble.

The guilt and bad habits formed in those early years. I was silent when the situation called for talking. These struggles always lay right below the surface and pop up with such unfortunate ease. Running away from a problem instead of facing it head-on was what my dad did best. Unfortunately, I mirrored this behavior.

My four years in high school were tough and filled with anger, to say the least. There were many fights and arguments with both parents. My mother called the police one night in my junior year because I was throwing things and she was scared. My father, of course, was not around. When the police arrived, one of the officers took me outside to talk to me. He said he had kids of his own and understood my anger. When I told him dad came home drunk all the time and it made me mad, he said I should have more patience because my dad works hard and a few drinks to relax him is not a bad thing. He said I should be more understanding. Then I tried to explain my mom was popping pills like they were candy. Again he responded that I should be understanding, trying to explain that my mom had a tough job as well, running the house with two children.

All these mixed messages left me with very negative feelings about myself. It is still a struggle to express my emotional or personal thoughts and feelings. I have strong and passionate opinions, but there is still that sick feeling in my stomach. I take Welbutrin (which I take for anxiety, and have for around 15 years), and sometimes when I am tired, or if I disagree during a heated discussion with someone I am close to, I feel like I am on the wrong side of the argument.

Now, I do know when I am calm that two people can disagree and there is no right or wrong. That is when I am feeling confident. It is when I am anxious about being abandoned, just because I have the wrong opinion, that I start sending mixed messages and discard any feeling I have on the subject to focus on the feelings of others and to back off and agree or stay mostly silent. This is about no one else, however. This is how I view me. That I don't feel loved or deserve love, that I have no confidence and feel my opinion doesn't count. When I reflect on my feelings, it is clear that I am more worried about what the other person thinks than I am connected to my true feelings. The sad part is that I have strong opinions but am too afraid to speak up.

Today I am aware of where I can go, and I am slowly working back to my own self, but it has taken a long time. Ignoring the old messages and replacing them with new ones. Still, when I am in the middle of an argument, I can start feeling belittled and almost hear the words of my mom or dad. "Kevin, you should keep all this to yourself or you should be more helpful," a major reason I never feel like I am doing enough. Just like when the police officer said that I should be understanding of my mother's sickness, my dad's drinking, my uncle's disability. Easy to get lost or confused when you are a kid self-parenting and pretty much raising your sister alone.

I mention my uncle's disability, and I should take a moment to fill you in on him. My uncle Billy was my mother's brother, and he lived with my grandmother until she was killed, as he was developmentally challenged. He was moved into a group home after that, and he actually improved his daily life skills and was able to make a life for himself. Perhaps my grandmother enabled him and he wasn't able to realize his full potential until he was away from her. We used to tease him, as he had a speech impediment, but he really seemed to love us. He was very kind and a really nice guy, something I remember well, and I do regret not getting a chance to know him better.

Growing up, my sister Melissa was left in my care most of the time. Good thing; because when her diapers needed changing or she needed to eat, I became the parent. She was born in 1960 when I was nine years old. Melissa remembers times that she would sit in wet diapers for a long time if I was not home to change her. When she was scared, my mom would tell her that it was too bad and suck it up. Needless to say, we were not comforted much as babies and small children.

We both remember being lost in a store more than once, and in one case I remember my mother saying it was my fault I got lost for not paying attention to where she was. She would also threaten to leave me in the store when I would keep asking her to buy a favorite food or toy. No wonder it took a long time to develop a taste for a favorite food or place, and why I still have feelings of abandonment.

The positive outcome in this story is my lifelong relationship with my sister. There has never been any sibling rivalry and we have a relationship that is based on trust. Melissa says it is probably because she has always regarded me as somewhat of a parent and caretaker. I may have viewed her as my child.

I recently asked her about one of her favorite memories of us as children and she reminded me of that each Saturday afternoon, she and I would have a bean and hotdog dinner together on trays in front of the television and watch the *Wide World of Sports.* Depending on the time of year, my mother would either make meals, or be in bed. In which case the meals fell to me; thankfully my grandmother taught me some cooking basics. My father was usually "working", even on Saturdays.

Trust was something of a rarity in my life and I am just now, in my marriage to Linda, trusting and believing enough in our relationship that she wants my honest opinions and feelings from my heart, not what I think I should feel. With that trust, it has been easier and I hope it will become more natural with practice. The problem is that the fear is deep, as the message I received growing up is that *I do not count.*

This was the ongoing banter that was pounded into my head from a very depressed mother. A mother I would take care of whenever she hid under the covers crying. I did this because I felt it was my job to take care of her, as my dad was not around much. Plus I was seeking her love, which was missing most my life. The messages were mixed; she would tell neighbors that I was a perfect boy and she loved me *beyond the moon.* But she would act quite differently when we were alone. I was invisible when my dad would stop drinking and show up for dinner, as all of her attention was directed to him. It was a strong feeling of abandonment when she did not need me. I was always at the ready, though; standing guard in case she did need me. Sometimes even now, I fight the anxiousness that crops up when I am needed to be helpful.

I look back now and remember how I would stay out later at night or watch television longer than usual. When I did stay out late, it usually consisted of me going to a movie alone, or going to a friend's house. I wasn't partying or getting into trouble, the idea was to stay out until my parents went to bed. They never asked if I did homework; I did it of course. I was a people pleaser and received plenty of positive feedback from my teachers, which was a significant amount of teachers with all the moving we did.

Of course, being a teacher's pet got me beat up a couple of times by the school bullies. I used to DJ the football rallies, and hung out with some football players. I remember there were two senior linemen, twin brothers, that kind of took me under their wings. I am not sure why- I think they thought I was funny. My mother would not go to the schools to defend me because we were staying under the radar in case of a quick needed getaway.

I was picked on all the time just for being a quiet kid, however I do remember several teachers saying I was funny but I never felt it. Maybe I was laughing off my pain.

As I mentioned, I never really partied in high school. I do remember getting drunk a couple of times, but I did not like the way I felt the next day. More especially, I did not want to be like my dad. Once, we were partying at a friend's house, and there was a kid who had a speech impediment. He reminded me of my uncle Billy, and we thought he was developmentally challenged, due to the way he spoke; a kind of indistinguishable mumble. We thought it would be funny to get him drunk, and after a while he passed out. An hour later he woke up yelling- but nobody could understand him. He passed out again, and we thought for sure he was dead. We went back and forth about what to do about him, and after a half hour, he suddenly sat up, mumbling again. This time we paid more attention, and we were more sober, and figured out that the whole night he was trying to say, "I have an abscessed tooth!"

I also remember singing in a school choir one year. My parents told me they would go, but my dad went drinking after work and because my mom could not drive, they did not show up. We moved to a new school the next year, and I decided not to join anything ever again.

In my junior and senior years of high school, I worked as a short order cook at a neighborhood restaurant. It was a family run restaurant that served everything from breakfast to ice cream, similar to a Friendly's Restaurant. I worked not to earn money, but to get out of the house as much as possible and have contact with people. I was lonely and starving for love, but I did not date much until my senior year, when I met a woman who also worked full time as a waitress at the restaurant. She was a year older and had graduated the year before. She was a shy, very nervous person with not a great deal of self confidence. Perfect for me to ride in on my white horse and rescue her. Perhaps I could then be confident in this endeavor.

She was Armenian, had long, dark hair and freckles. Her father was a mailman, and I don't remember much about her mother. After a couple of months we got married and stayed married for a year. I do not know why, but my mother was thrilled for us. She just loved this woman and maybe that was why I felt after a few months that I had made a serious mistake. She reminded me of my mother, so I guess it was familiar to me. I found her very clingy, and dependent on me, and that eventually dragged me down. She needed a lot of nurturing, and I did not have it to give to her. After I graduated high school, I left her and I moved to Boston.

I did not receive any help from my parents, as my mother hated the idea of me moving away. I got a small apartment in Boston and a job as a short order cook at a diner around the corner in Government Center. I applied and was accepted into the Northeast Broadcasting school. I had not yet filed for a divorce because my parents asked me to wait awhile to be sure, however I had started a relationship with a woman that came into the diner for breakfast every day. She had a great sense of humor and carried herself with confidence. She knew I was married and unhappy, and I was attracted to her because she struck me as a strong person. Somehow my mother got wind of the relationship and knew I would stay at this woman's house on Saturday nights.

One night, mom showed up outside this woman's apartment with my wife and caused an unpleasant scene, walking down the street shouting my name. Now, this woman I was seeing lived with her parents in an apartment in a neighborhood, so she urged me to stop my mother before the neighbors called the police. So we both went out to talk to my mother, who was standing there with my wife. My mother shouted at the girl, saying that I was married, and that I should stay married and finish what I started. I think she wanted it more than I, or my wife, did. During this whole awkward encounter, my wife did not say a word. My mother thought that by confronting me, it was the best way to get me to see her point of view. It did not, as I filed for divorce that very next Monday. The other woman stopped seeing me at the same time, saying she was not ready to deal with my crazy mother. My wife did not contest the divorce but my mother tried to speak at the proceeding. She kept yelling at the judge, saying, "I want to speak", and "what the hell do you know about my son?" The judge had to have her removed from the courtroom when she refused to be quiet.

I did not have much contact with my mom and dad after that. A friend told me that my dad spent most of his time with my ex-wife after the divorce because she was so broken up, but I always thought there might have been more to the relationship. That would not have shocked me in the least, as he would often brag to me that he was a ladies' man.

My mom tried the same tactic with my sister years later when she would not leave her boyfriend's house and come home. She went to the local police station and asked them to go pick her up and bring her home. When they refused, she went out back of the police station and tried to steal a police car to go after Melissa herself. They were kind enough to call me to bring her home and not press charges.

I worked for one of my cousin's husbands while I was in college; he owned a sandwich shop and one of my responsibilities was to close. I used to drop money and receipts off at his home after closing on Friday and Saturday nights. One Saturday, I had a serious accident while driving to his house. On the way, a car crossed the center line and hit the driver's side of my car head on and kept going, ripping the door off my vehicle. Needless to say, I was frazzled. How I wasn't seriously injured, I will never know. I remember saying I was fine, when I knew I wasn't. In my mind, I blamed myself for what happened so I did not want any help. My inner shame led me to quit my job. I did not look at it as an accident, I thought it was all my fault. After that night, the communication between my cousin and I was minimal, and we lost touch soon after that when I got my first radio job and moved to New Hampshire.

Around town it was common knowledge that my mother had severe episodes of depression and she told us she was diagnosed with manic depression, now referred to as bipolar disorder. Needless to say, she could be a bit crazy and out of control. In the winter, she would stay in bed days on end, sleeping and feeling depressed. It was during these times that I would be at her bedside being the diligent caretaker.

When she was taking her Lithium regularly or in the summer, Mom was energetic and happy and you could not get her to sit down. As a child, this was very confusing, so I would become invisible and try to stay out of the way. On a couple of occasions in the past, she was committed to a hospital by my dad and her doctor. I was only a baby the first time and around three the second time she was committed.

When I was older, my grandmother told me that mom was treated with shock therapy in the hospital.

At one point I counted nineteen prescription bottles on the kitchen table. I remember my sister Melissa telling me that Mom was upset with her for smoking pot as a teen. Mom was afraid marijuana was a gateway drug and she would start using other drugs, like heroin. Her response was that she never had to go elsewhere for drugs, as there were plenty to be found in her own home. After that, Mom never brought it up again.

I did not know much about my mom's past, and what I did know happened after she met my dad. She was in her teens when her father died, and no one ever talked about what happened. My mom said she worked as a detective for a major Boston department store but no one ever said which one, because nobody ever spoke about it and if I asked Gram or my aunt they would always respond, *ask her.*

Mom and Dad met on a blind date in Salem NH, and married shortly after in June of 1949. I don't know anything else about their courtship or life before I was born, as they never spoke of their prior life. Mom would only say that Dad was charming and handsome. The only other comment she made was that a few times Dad had picked her up for a date, Gram never knew he was *a bit tipsy.* She thought it was cute.

Laughter and affection between my parents was far and few between. When my mother had her downswings, my father would stay longer at work, or just leave. It was up to me to take care of my mother during these times, as avoidance was a skill my father had mastered.

She also loved his sense of humor, ironically a skill he developed as a morning radio DJ in Springfield MA.

He had a great radio voice for those early days of broadcasting; deep and authoritative. When the station moved to Boston, his job was given to someone else. He never said why, and he may not have been told why, but my Dad left broadcasting and never returned. I remember him talking about the job and I came to the conclusion that he likely missed that career and that it was a huge disappointment in his life. He went to work for an auto parts store in South Boston as an accountant.

I recall one time driving to work with him on St. Patrick's Day 1959. His office was right on Broadway in South Boston where a huge St. Patrick's Day parade was held every year. I sat on his desk looking out the window and remember three things distinctly: loud marching bands, piercing voices and dad and his co-workers drinking, cheering excessively for a charismatic man who looked up at us, waved and smiled as he walked by. My dad said that there was talk that the man may run for President. His name was John F. Kennedy.

Like most people my age and older, I remember when Kennedy was shot. I heard it on the school intercom, which was an old brown box on the wall. They dismissed school, and I remember feeling sad; as everyone talked about what a good president he was, and that he was kind. I came home and saw my mother sitting on the couch, crying. Two days later, I was staying at my grandmother's house and had just turned the TV on when I saw Jack Ruby shoot Lee Harvey Oswald. I remember that moment more vividly than anything else at the time.

Dad somehow lasted twenty years at his job in spite of *several long vacations,* as my mom would call them, in and out of hospitals getting sober. He did get fired for stealing money from the company, but a deal was worked out for him to pay it back, so no charges were filed.

His next job was a tax assessor for the State of Massachusetts. My dad had a great love of music and it was one of the few subjects that he would talk to me about. This was, again, a time when I felt

27

a rare connection to my dad. I can now look back and see how he unknowingly played a big role in my choices with both healthy and unhealthy behavior.

On the positive side he talked about artists and music he loved growing up and would play them for me, or we would listen to a radio station that played older tunes. I ended up liking most of his music as much as the current top 40 hits playing on the radio.

Dad was friendly with a few Boston DJ's and he once took me to see one of them on the air. I was only around eleven but I remember being so excited and thinking that I wanted to do this when I grew up.

When Dad would drink and argue with Mom, I would shut myself in my room, put on ear phones and play music loudly to block out the noise. Any money I had would be spent on purchasing music. At that time, 45's played on record players were big, and I had two small plastic record players and a large collection of current hits and oldies. I would sit and do my own personal radio show for hours, using the newspaper to read headlines and weather between songs.

Doing this to avoid my parents fighting could be considered negative but something positive came out of it; after graduation from a Boston broadcasting school I got a radio job in Warwick, Rhode Island. The station was very small- in fact, it was in the dining room of a house. The general manager lived in the house, and his bedroom was right down a small hall from the studio. While I was on the air in the morning, he would come out of his bedroom and into the kitchen, which was attached to the dining room/station. So while I was on the air, he was cooking breakfast and making coffee just feet away. I lasted about a year before taking a job at a small station in Nashua, New Hampshire. My audition consisted of announcing a few songs, reading news headlines and the weather forecast (sound familiar?). I remember the station program director could not believe I had not been on the radio before, and I got the job.

Another way I escaped the yelling and fighting was to sit or lay outside. I would study the colors, clouds, and the flow of the wind. I ordered a large wall chart that listed the names and descriptions of all the different clouds we see. It hung on my wall and I memorized all the names and the weather they produced. My interest in weather blossomed from there, and another one of my escapes turned into a thirty-year career.

*Linda's Story*

*"Sometimes a person has to go back, really back, to have a sense, an understanding of all that's gone to make then, before they can go forward".*

Paule Marshall

*Remembering the early years...*

I was born on January 23, 1960 in New London, Connecticut. My hospital birth picture shows me holding my chin like I was in deep thought; I guess I came out thinking. Baby pictures also showed I was well cared for, well dressed, and always looked so cute. I think my mother was around for my first year, but got sick again after my younger brother was born. My mom spent most of my younger years in the Connecticut state hospital in Norwich, and my dad would seek help from babysitters to care for us kids. I vaguely remember trips to the psychiatric hospital, or mental hospital, as it was so often referred. I have one memory of all of us sitting in the hospital courtyard on a cement bench and another memory of my mom coming home some weekends on furloughs, and my dad having to take her back. I remember not wanting her to leave and crying.

My mom was one of the first people in our town to open our home to female prisoners on furloughs. Our home town of Niantic was also home to the state of Connecticut's female prison. The prisoners were getting ready to be released and needed the community experiences. I remember a female prisoner in our living room, ironing. My mom also must have been doing well at that point, to be able to open our home to these women.

I also had been given a shirt that my mom wore when she was a den mother for boy scouts, I believe for my older brother. This makes me think that she must have had some healthy stretches and did some wonderful civic volunteering. I have spent much of my career doing community work, and I often wonder if she had the same passion when she was well.

I remember the day she died. It was a sunny day, on August 10, 1967. We were at the beach with a babysitter. When we came home, there was a big black car in our driveway, which was the car from the church. I remember feeling an immediate, overwhelming sense of sadness; I remember thinking that my mom had died and it was true. She was gone. She had been telling my dad for a while that he should divorce her and find us a "new mother". She had been committed to the state hospital and felt her children needed a mother who could be home to nurture them.

My dad was dedicated to her, for better or worse, and would not consider divorce. Which led her to take matters into her own hands. She somehow escaped the secure hospital unit and ran into the nearby highway, throwing herself in front of a big Mack truck and was killed instantly. My dad told us later that the truck driver was an emotional mess and blamed himself, despite my dad offering him support. I often wonder how his life turned out and if he was able to forgive himself. I would have liked to have met him, yet knew that would never be possible, as my mom's death was rarely talked about.

To this day, I cannot remember if I attended my mother's funeral. I have asked my dad many times, and he reminds me, but for some reason I am unable to retain the answer. It is mostly a blur, but I do remember the house being full of people after the service and a large amount of food and conversation.

My mother tried to take her life other times. I had heard she tried at home when we were with her, but I do not remember. My dad did say she would call him at times while he was at work and say he better come home quickly or she may hurt us. I do not remember anything she may have said or done, only the stories from my dad.

About eleven years ago, in 2004, my mother's sister, Aunt Marie, gave me a box filled with letters and notes retrieved from my mom's hospital bedside drawer. Also in the box was the den mother's shirt that my mother once wore, and I feel so fortunate she gave these items to me. In an attached note, My Aunt Marie wrote: *I hate to part with it, (the shirt), but it is time to let go. Please take good care of the shirt and keep it close to your heart. Think of your mom as a dear, sweet, and loving person. Please talk to her as if she was near. She hears you.*

The notes and letters are very dear to me as well. I have read them a few times and have tried to make sense of them, to understand my mom's thought process. Some letters and notes are very clear and others not; some very dark and others light. I soon realized it did not really matter that I understood them, they are very precious pieces of my mom's thoughts and feelings. I swell with emotion just looking at them. I feel happy and comforted thinking my mom touched that piece of paper and I feel sad seeing her deep struggles reflected in ink. They are incredible reflections of her thoughts and feelings at one given moment, whatever those moments were to her. She processed past events in her life, focusing on things that still bothered her, almost seeming to obsess about some things. Her letters showed she cared deeply about fairness, staying objective, kindness, and sticking up for those she loved  dearly, like her sister Marie.  My mom was heavily medicated and had shock treatments, which she disliked.  I know this type of therapy is still being used and may be effective for some people. My guess is that back in those days, they were less humane and it was done without much compassion.

Some of the letters found in My mom's hospital drawer were written to her children or her dear sister Marie. These letters and notes were obviously never sent or read while she was alive, for which I am thankful for today. One letter, written on June 2, 1966 to her sister said, *I thought it would be a good idea to send my dear sis a line to tell her how much better I am, really. I feel as if a big weight has been lifted and I am a person, the person, that I was a long time ago- I cannot explain it but it is (the feeling) –that feeling that I've been born again...and It is a pretty nice feeling! My love to you and everyone...XXXXXXX, Anne.*

Another unsent letter was to my dad, my siblings and me addressed *Dear John and all my dear cubs.* She thanks us for sending handmade cards that she loved to look at, and thanks a friend for sending a card that is *a ray of sunshine to those that are getting well.* Another note says *I want to go home to my husband and family, please. No place but home- I never felt as miserable away from home, so many days without my family or husband.*

One scribble says *A pause between one life and another.* On the same piece of brown stained paper she writes about closing our eyes and feeling with our heart. Her wisdom is amazing, albeit in scribbles and often with words written on top of each other as if she missed moving down a line. In one letter she writes about children and how they are spoken to: *The emotional thinking and habits of a child- their way of being in the world- whatever said, should be said in respect for their feelings- they have feelings and self-respect no matter how small they are and a sense of well-being can be definitely traced to this respect given them- to let them know glad they exist instead of being burden(s). It is their world-*

*though a tiny one, nevertheless, it is all to them.* That letter means the most to me, as I have done years of work in the field of child protective services. I feel so sad when I have a case where the children are perceived as burdens and a "drag" to raise. It's so painful and heart wrenching for me to witness children often thought of as an inconvenience to someone in their own family.

Another long letter apologizes for my mom *being so selfish*, although she says she was selfish for the *best of intentions.* She said she was only trying to get to the *truth of a situation.* Another scribble reads: *Besides, the tree of life is too beautiful with all its wonderful fruits to be infected by disgusting crawling worms.* Another note along those dark lines: *A worm rarely picks on bad apples...His satisfaction would not be quite as gratifying.*

In yet another note, she asks if the medicine is making her eyes blurry, and she writes that she is in treatment at *Kettle's Treatment, Ward 3* and she is falling more: *this (treatment) makes me walk very awkward and I trip- I have proof from the marks on my knees.* She continues on... *I appreciate your efforts to make me feel better- the fastest and fairest way would be to let me go home, since this doesn't happen at home (check with my hubby.)* So it seems, a perfect time for me to go back home.

At age seven, my mom's death was a very sad and confusing time. These letters, stories I have been told, and only a few memories fill my heart and my head to this day.

For a few years, my dad raised us alone. He was born in Italy and came to America when he was eighteen. He learned English and was a remarkable mason, making beautiful brick and stone creations. He is a strong man of character and faith, and instilled those values in his children. My brothers and I have many memories of these years with my dad. I remember we had a simple dinner schedule; every week was the same. One night was chicken from the corner store in a little paper bag, another night was grinders, another steak. Some nights we would wake my dad up by putting our hamster down his shirt. He worked us around the house and yard as his little laborers and he did a remarkable job holding us all together. I will always believe my dad is the one reason why all of us have done well in life.

When I was nine, my dad met and married Carol after a short courtship. He and my stepmother are still married today and going strong.

My stepmom had a troubled childhood and had just come out of the convent when my dad met her in 1969. She had been a nun for ten years, and she brought structure and rules to our home. We had serious chores, tons of rules and a tight schedule. Gone were the days of watching *Dark Shadows* after school and eating Devil Dogs with the neighborhood kids. Looking back, she was exactly what we needed, although I did not think so at the time. Being the only girl, she would bring me in from kickball games, building tree forts and log cabins, and from riding banana bikes to the pond to catch frogs. She wanted me to be *more of a girl* and had me focus on such chores like cooking, sewing and cleaning. It was too late though; I was happy outside playing kickball and building forts. I guess I was a feminist back then, as well.

We lived on a wonderful street with lots of neighborhood kids, woods, and we had great outdoor fun. One thing I am so thankful for to this day is my stepmom's attitude towards my mom. My dad had dated a woman, with whom he was quite serious with, that told him that when they married there would be no mention of my mother and no pictures of her around. My dad dumped her after that. My stepmom felt differently, and allowed pictures of my mom and occasionally would talk about her. I will forever be grateful for her respect. If not for her, the memory of my mom may have been snuffed out completely and I would not be writing this book. I would not have had the chance to weave the memory of my mom into my life, and I am not sure where that would have left me emotionally. I hope my stepmother understands my gratitude for that gift.

By my early teen years, I began drinking. I found enjoyment in getting drunk and being wild, which made me forget everything. I was a straight A student, a good athlete and had many friends. My life was filled with working, which I did from a young age. I reluctantly went to church, loved going to the beach, huge music concerts and volunteering. I loved taking care of my baby brother, who was eleven years younger. I would take him to the beach to skip stones. However, drinking gave me an outlet different from all the rest, I could feel crazy and free. My first experience of getting drunk was on a farm where my brothers and I worked for years. A customer brought in homemade blackberry brandy, and a co-worker and I drank it in the cooler, finishing the whole big bottle in one night. I was probably around thirteen or fourteen. I looked forward to drinking on weekends when I could, and sometimes even before school. Drinking made me feel happy and free.

One of the adults who owned a house on the farm would leave us his house key, and would even leave us booze. This was fun, but obviously very inappropriate of him as I look back now. My parent's strictness probably kept me out of trouble, as well as some good luck. There were firm expectations from my parents' that I would keep up my high grades, do well at work, attend church and do my home chores. I had a significant amount of conflict with my stepmom as a teenager, as we really struggled to understand each other. I spent a lot of time with friends, had some crazy times and probably could have gotten into trouble. Without getting into great details, suffice it to say I partied with my friends often, kept up my other responsibilities, and managed to do well overall. Looking back now, I definitely could have used some counseling as a teen, although because I functioned well, it never came to light.

However, I still had a secret that was too hard to talk about without severe anxiety and angst. Few friends knew the truth about my mother. I was too embarrassed to tell many people and felt ashamed. I had to dance around this truth in most situations, and it was uncomfortable. I would feel anxious when the subject of mothers came up and would physically sweat and feel nauseated. At the same time, I deeply craved the opportunity to talk about her. I wished for the strength and the courage to know how to, without feeling embarrassed. These opportunities never came until much later in life.

I think it is this inner struggle that started my passion to break through the barriers of shame and stigma, although I did not know it then. There was a wall between me and the rest of the world regarding my mother's death. Little did I know, my whole career and life itself would be fueled by this intense desire to break down these walls, helping myself and others speak their truth without shame and fear.

# 3

## BLIZZARD CONDITIONS

### *Choices Along the Way*

*A blizzard is considerable falling, blowing snow that reduces visibility to a point where the sky, air and ground become indistinguishable---everything is white.*

*Kevin's Story...*

People caught in a whiteout can become completely disoriented and lose their way, sometimes with serious consequences. This is a strong feeling I had in my personal life as I went out on my own into the world. I felt lost most of the time. When it was just me I was happy enough, but quickly felt a great deal of loneliness. I was a fixer and my addiction was to fix or rescue my partners. In my own mind I had no value unless I was saving my girlfriends. From what, I did not know.

Looking back, most of the time I picked women that had the same qualities of, and acted like, my mother. Women with significant highs and lows. The unpredictable behavior and the way my dad introduced me to sex also seemed to attract me to women who did not want a serious relationship and lived on what some would call *the other side of the tracks*. This lasted from my late teens to late twenties. Casual relationships that I look back on now with a bit of shame and maybe some guilt. What bothers me the most is how little self-esteem I had for myself. I was in one relationship at a time, but the time was short and while I was always loyal during those years, my partners were seeing other men and being very open about it. I was fine with that because I felt I did not deserve to be special in their eyes. It is a weird contrast for me now, but it felt a bit exciting to me. My dad was cheating on my mom all the time, so I wanted to be more honest in my relationships.

As I got into my thirties I wanted to make better choices, but my second marriage was with a women who, while lovely in many ways , was in need of a rescue. My love for her was based mostly on how I could fix her broken heart and make her feel good about herself again. Once I thought I had accomplished that, I lost all interest. When we met in 1972, I was working as a music director for a country radio station owned by her dad in Worcester, Massachusetts. She was working as the receptionist to help out her dad, and had just returned from New York City after a bad relationship break up.

She also worked as a clothes buyer for a major department store and was, it seemed, very good at it. We worked together once a week picking songs to play on the radio station and I thought it was cool we had the same taste in music. It was fun,  we got to know each other and we started dating a month or two after I started working there. She was eight or nine years older than me and could not understand my interest in her. I thought she was very attractive but it was turning her sadness into happiness that was the real reason I was falling in love with her.

I was hired as the music director and afternoon DJ. For some reason, Thursday was the day we changed the music lineup. So on Monday through Wednesday I would listen to new music and choose what went on the lineup. One time, she was walking by

40

when I was playing a song, and mentioned how much she liked it. All I could think was "this song sucks". So I asked her what she liked about the song, and that started a new relationship of us picking songs together. I agreed to put the song on the lineup, and it became a fairly big hit for a singer named Dolly Parton and a song called *Lonely Comin' Down*.

When the station hired me the ratings were low; they were the number six station out of seven in the area. A year later the station was moved to the recently opened Worcester Mall and was the number two station in the market. We brought concerts to town and had a fun on-air line-up. I worked the 2 PM To 6PM time slot and this huge turn around allowed her Dad to sell the station and move home to Maine.

We got married and moved to Maine with him, her mom and younger sister in 1974. I got a morning job at a country radio station in Presque Isle and she started an ad agency with her mom and dad. I also voiced their clients' radio and TV ads. It was a good living, I enjoyed the work and was becoming well known in the area. My wife, however, was not happy. She missed being a buyer, so we packed up and moved to Phoenix, Arizona in 1976 so she could pursue her career.

She got a job as a buyer for a large West Coast department store and I found work at a sports station. I did some on-air commercials, but most of the time I was an engineer; meaning I was just sitting and mostly punching buttons during Phoenix Suns NBA basketball games and Phoenix Giants baseball games, the farm team of the San Francisco Giants.

She loved her job and I hated mine. I worked nights, while she worked days and traveled almost every week to Los Angeles for at least one or two overnights, which was not good for such an insecure guy like me. We had a great apartment in Scottsdale; it had a pool, a game room and most of the people were around our age. I chose to isolate myself in the apartment and started to feel very depressed. I missed being on air and I wanted to get into TV and weather, but did not have enough experience to get TV work in a big city. I knew, for me at least, our marriage was in trouble. My wife was getting overwhelmed with work and was missing her family, so in 1979 we moved back to Presque Isle.

This time I worked a morning show at a hit music station. I also spent my spare time with her Dad. He treated me like a son and was happy I married his daughter, as he felt she would have likely been single, so I was a savior to him. A perfect fit for my role as the fixer. He owned a beautiful piece of land in the area and had built a cabin at the top of a big hill that looked out over a huge valley. Every day I would see deer, moose and bear walking around with their young. It was a very peaceful place to me. Her dad and I planted corn and potatoes and would bring their dog, an old and cranky soul, but I loved him and spent every day taking him on long walks. He loved to chase squirrels but had arthritis and could barely run. His age caught up with him and he died one night in my father-in-law's basement. Everyone was sad of course, but I was heartbroken. I remember sitting alone in the basement with him in front of me and crying for hours. We buried him up on the hill and I would visit him every day. I decided not to ever have another dog again so I would never have to suffer such a painful loss. The thought of all the happiness he brought me was completely lost to me after he died.

My first son Jeff was born in 1981. Because of my early hours I could spend a lot of time with him as a baby, but the down side was I never saw his mother. She was not a morning person, so she slept until 9 or 10 AM and left for work around 11. She would eat lunch with her mother, they would watch soap operas till 4

PM, then work until 7 or 8 PM. Because I went to work early in the morning, I would be in bed when she got home so we did not see much of each other. On the weekends she would sleep all morning and did not talk when she first woke. She then spent the rest of the day shopping with her sister and our son.

Many weekend nights I was working as a DJ for high school dances and special events, birthdays, weddings or reunions. This left little time for bonding as a couple, and it felt like we were living separate lives, though she seemed quite happy with this arrangement. When I would bring these feelings up, she answered by saying that I was way too sensitive, and there was some truth to that. I was very needy because of the insecurity I felt about not being loveable. I now know that speaking up about feelings is important and not to give up if someone does not understand where you are coming from. I also understand the importance of listening to the feelings that the other person is dealing with, and not rush to judgment or run possible fixes in my mind while the other person is talking, because I stop listening and miss a lot.

This has been a very hard concept for me to grasp. It was a huge struggle for Linda and I as well, and still can be if I am not paying attention. When I was told I was too sensitive, I would feel very angry and resentful, isolate myself in a room or stay late at work. I would be very quiet when we were in the same space, and if I talked to her at all it was in a very cold or nasty tone. I was very hurt but did not know it then. I was craving the attention I did not get as a kid and reverted to acting like one.

So I turned my attention to my work. Doing this often made me quite good at my job, and each new job was a better one with an increase in pay and professional confidence. My personal life on the other hand was a disaster.

One late summer afternoon in 1982 my father-in-law and I were working in the garden when he felt a sharp pain in his chest. When it did not go away after a couple of days, a trip to the doctors and some tests revealed advanced and inoperable cancer. His health went downhill very quickly in spite of a trip to a clinic in Atlanta for treatment. He died only seven months later, and the family was devastated. My wife took it especially hard because they were so close. I could not be there for her because it was such a shock and loss for me. From that point on what little was left of our relationship fell apart.

In 1984, when my son was three, we divorced and I moved back to Worcester to work at a different radio station and at the only TV station, Channel 27. On TV, I worked the hourly news updates 4 to 11 PM. Then I worked nights at the radio station from midnight to 5 AM. I did not see my son much. He would come and spend two weeks in the summer, and I would drive to Presque Isle for Thanksgiving to spend three days with him. We would spend a vacation week together in the fall and that was it.

My ex-wife was very angry with me for leaving and would abruptly cut my visits short. This was sad and hurtful but I did not speak up, as I felt so much guilt for leaving and felt I was a bad father who did not deserve to see Jeff more than I already was able.

At that time, I never considered how it felt for my son or its effects on him. I was not aware enough to be able to see any point of view other than my own. My only worry was what it meant to me. Putting this on paper is very painful and fills me with regret that I was not a stronger person for my son.

In 1986, I had a chance to return to Presque Isle to work full time on a show called *Chamber Magazine* for the only TV station in town, Channel 8. It was a local *60 Minutes* type show. I was traveling all over northern and eastern Maine to various out of the way interesting places and talking to people working unusual or extraordinary jobs.

I was also a co-host of an early morning show in the Fall called *Potato Pickers Special.* It allowed me to do interviews with Maine's political figures and talk to farmers on air about the weather, progress and challenges with harvesting their crops. It was a show to help farmers to schedule picking according to the weather forecast. I took the job to be closer to my son and to be able to continue working in television.

Not long after I took the job, my ex-wife and my son moved to Bangor. After her father's death the ad agency started losing clients and she needed to find work. I tried to get work in Bangor but nothing was available.

Something did happen at Channel 8 in 1987 that gave my weather career a boost. It is ironic, but the 6 and 11 PM weather forecaster did not own a TV, even though he was on TV. He arrived at work one Wednesday afternoon and announced he no longer wanted to report the weather as of that Friday. He was a farmer and wanted to devote full time to his crops. The station was in a panic. I offered to fill in while they searched for his replacement, and being in a bind they agreed. What nobody expected was that I quickly caught on with viewers, and the news director and station manager were surprised at my ease in front of the camera on live television. They could tell I was really enjoying myself. I don't know why I never applied for the position, but they offered me the job and my television weather career was launched.

In late 1988, I was driving to visit friends in Worcester but stopped in Portland to see old Channel 8 friends who were working at WCSH 6. They told me a weather job had just opened and introduced me to the News Director. We hit it off and he had me do a taped audition. I stopped back a few days later after my Worcester visit and, much to my surprise, was offered the job.

I worked the last two weeks, Monday through Friday, at Channel 8 then drove to Portland to do all the weekend shows at Channel 6 morning, noon and evenings. Channel 6 also owned WLBZ 2 in Bangor and would run the broadcasts out of Portland. The broadcast was also on cable Channel 2, which was seen in northern Maine, so many of my old Channel 8 viewers tuned in. I think that helped a bit with the ratings increase on The Morning Report once Lee Nelson and I teamed up in 1990.

I bought a car for the move, and it was my first experience with a stick shift. I stalled it at every toll booth on the way to Portland. I found an apartment within walking distance of the station so I did not have to do much driving. I continued to do all the weekend news shows, as well as Monday and Tuesday morning's weather.

On Wednesdays I went out in the field to do reports for a series called *People, Places and Things.* Another chance to travel to out of the way locations all over Maine and New Hampshire. During this time I was back to dating different women; nothing serious, just casual.

In 1991 I met my third wife; we were married not long after we met and had a son, Taylor, in 1992. I was asked to devote full time to weather forecasting on News Center's Morning Report. The show, which had been thirty minutes, was expanded to one hour. New equipment was bought with better forecasting tools and the ability to make maps that were more colorful and easy to read for the viewer. It was a very exciting time of growth in this field and I came in on the ground floor. I was very happy at work, and even with a wife, I was feeling lonely in my personal life. I was extremely happy we had a baby and with my Morning Show hours, I could spend plenty of time with him in the afternoon. We lived in an apartment in Portland, and when the neighbors above us moved out and left behind a few pet snakes, some alive some dead, we decided it was time to buy our own house. We moved to a neighborhood off Ocean Avenue in Portland next door to Linda, her then husband and two daughters in 1993.

Our children played together all the time. Linda and I would talk in the afternoon while the kids played. I did not know what was going on with me at the time, but I was having periods of depression. Other than ACOA(Adult Children of Alcoholics) Meetings, I had never done any therapy. My sad feelings were becoming overwhelming and my wife was unhappy. Of course my efforts to fix that were not working well, and I was feeling hopeless, so I started a personal journey of self-awareness.

My early expectations were that I would fix what was wrong with me. Kind of like repairing a gimpy knee with an operation and get on with my life with newfound joy and happiness for not only me, but my wife as well. To my shock and dismay, I had to sink lower before climbing out of the despair I was feeling.

My journey was not a miracle cure. Actually, it was not a cure at all. It was a very slow process and a growing awareness of how bad I really felt about myself a good deal of the time. I discovered that dealing with my sadness led me to blame others for my unhappiness. It was not all on me. but I kept choosing partners that I thought had their own unresolved issues. Now, this is not meant as a judgment of my past partners. I am speaking about my perception of the situations and relationships, and I am sure my partners may see it differently. They were not bad people in any way; it is clear to me now that we were just mismatched.

*Linda's Story*

*Your diamonds are not in far distant mountains or in yonder seas;
they are in your own backyard, if you but dig for them.*

Russell H. Conwell

I have never been one to regret my decisions. I feel we all make choices that are right for us at that time in our life and we need to accept and live with what we have chosen. This is not always easy but so important to me. This chapter is about some of the major choices I made along the way that were not the smartest. I made them without understanding myself fully or not listening to myself. To some readers, these choices may seem comparatively insignificant. Others may be horrified. They are just some of the choices that influenced my life course. Like we all do, I have woven those choices into my life and accept them fully as part of my journey to where I am today. Acceptance is a key part of *embracing one's shame,* as I like to say.

After high school, I went to college at the University of Southern Maine and studied social work and criminal justice. I could not decide which major I liked best, so I graduated magna cum laude with a dual major. I had many fond memories and wonderful times in college and met some amazing friends. I was over three hours away from my home in Connecticut, which seemed just the right distance. I could go home when it was a holiday, yet it felt far enough away to give me freedom.

During my sophomore year, I went on a student exchange to Boise State University in Idaho and ended up meeting and living with an Iranian man for the summer, during the Iranian crisis no less.

We hiked all the beautiful places in Idaho and surrounding areas. I told my parents I truly loved this man and we were going to get married and spend half our time in the United States and half in Iran. They thought I was crazy, but I was determined to make it work. The relationship ended when I came back east and along with it the very impossible dream of going between two countries during a major international crisis. This is an experience my family still teases me about to this day.

College was another time where I knew my mother's suicide was still unresolved in my heart and mind. I would get a lump in my throat and feel anxious in social work classes when the topic of suicide came up, and I was so afraid to bring up the subject. My advisor in social work once said to me that he sensed something wasn't quite right with me but he did not know what it was about. My first respond was *oh my God*. I was so afraid he would think less of me and that I shouldn't do social work if he knew my mother committed suicide. I even remember where we were standing when he told me he sensed something was going on with me. Looking back, it was such a missed opportunity on my part to talk to him about my life and fears, but I was still too afraid. On the outside, I was happy and did great in school and in my internships. On the inside, I still had so much anxiety concerning my mom's suicide. It was not a constant feeling, but came up often enough that I should have paid attention to it and sought help. After all, I was studying social work.

College was also when I freely dated men and had my first sexual experiences. I had tremendous guilt after my first experience due to my Catholic upbringing. I was not sure if I would be struck down by lightning or something even worse. I had nightmares about having sex before I "should have". The guilt was overwhelming for a while, but it subsided and I enjoyed the college life of dating and partying. I graduated with very good grades, and many great memories.

After college, I fulfilled another dream of joining the Peace Corps. I was sent to Sierra Leone, West Africa to work with rice farmers. I was among a great group of volunteers and we were very close. That experience was a challenge and filled with irreplaceable memories. This was so important to me as I have always craved challenges and unique experiences. It was also lonely at times and difficult work.

In the early days, I started dating an African man who was one of our teachers in the training village. He was very fluent in English, extremely sophisticated for his country, and intelligent. He was also sweet and funny. We dated the entire two years I was there and we decided he would come back to the United States with me at the end of my term. I asked my family to support his visa, and they wisely said no. We got engaged in Sierra Leone so he could then come to the U.S. on a fiancé visa, and we would have ninety days to marry once we got to the U.S. I secretly had many doubts about this and questioned myself on many occasions. Was this what I really wanted to do? Did I really love him or was I caught up in the planning and the excitement of it all? What about the men I still thought about back in the U.S.? Regardless of these doubts and questions, I did it anyway and I arrived home in Connecticut engaged to a man my family had never met, who was from a completely different world and culture. I wasn't sure if we would settle in Connecticut or Maine; although I said we would go to wherever I got a job first. I quickly was offered a job in Portland, Maine, so off we went to start our life there.

It was not long before I knew I had made a mistake. Not with the man I married, as he was a very good man. The mistake was within myself. I had not listened to my inner doubts and feelings, my inner voice. I did not really want to marry him and I was not ready for marriage. How could I know this in my heart but not listen to it? How could I have not connected my inner self with my actions? I was back home, wanted my freedom and wanted to reconnect with old boyfriends. Although I had these feelings, I was still faithful to the relationship. I struggled with this as the year went on. I brought back this man from Africa, married him and now he was totally dependent on me as he learned about our culture, even though he was an independent man. He was new to this country and there were so many adjustments. Eventually, one of my dear friends said I should try counseling, as I was in a bind and needed help and guidance.

Needless to say, counseling was life changing for me. Maybe because the counselor was an incredible woman who could quickly recognize my struggle. She barely talked about my current dilemma; she immediately asked if I had ever sorted out my childhood issues. I replied "no", and started crying uncontrollably.

I did find the strength to tell my husband I wanted a divorce. He was devastated at first. I still tried to support him while he found his own place and began to build his life without me. He did amazingly well after a while and I felt less guilt as time went on. I learned so much about myself in counseling and the reasons why I made certain choices. I found relief in understanding why I did what I did and desperately wanted to learn from it. I knew I had hurt my new husband, but I mostly hurt myself by not listening to that loud inner voice that knew my true feelings.

Like many young people in their twenties, I worked hard and played even harder. My job in social work as a child protective worker was incredibly difficult. This was a job I was so grateful to have had, as it helped form who I am today. It is the first time I worked in a job that had to balance compassion and toughness, where you had to sometimes go to court and remove children, often amidst anger, sadness and disbelief. I had to believe in myself and the reasons I was doing this work. This job helped me be clear about my feelings, and understand that sometimes things are really tough to do, but yet are still the right choices. I was connecting the deep emotions that came up in that position with my actions. I have always been a deep thinker and feeler, so that part wasn't new. What was new was that I learned to listen to myself and to understand the reason I was doing what I was doing, whether it be personal or professional. Simply put, I learned to believe in myself, listen to what I was feeling, and do what I needed to do to make something better.

By my late twenties, I had dated a lot of men, had many one night stands and traveled around. I am quite certain that it was comfortable to be carefree with men because it was easier than being committed. Deep down I was very afraid of being abandoned or being stuck in a commitment, as I later learned in counseling. I still struggle with these feelings at times.

Some of the choices I made then scare me now, such as going off for weekends with men I had just met. A few times, I went away with men whose last name I did not even know. They seemed really nice and were usually lots of fun. I remember one of my dear friends and roommates talking to me about her fears for not only me, but for her. She asked me to be more careful about the men I brought home to our apartment, as I would bring guys home that I had just met and it scared her. She worried I might bring home a murderer. She asked me if I ever worried about that, and of course I said no. I respected her feelings very much, so I became more careful, as she was my dear close friend and I did not want her to be scared. However, I still took some horrible chances with men and ended up in a few bad places. My dad always said my mom was a special angel on my shoulder, and he had no idea how true that was. I still believe my mom is my angel; protecting me and she probably tried hard during those times to send me some signs that I foolishly ignored.

By my late twenties, I was ready to make some changes. I decided to become celibate after a particularly crazy week and was beginning to feel like I wanted more in terms of relationships than casual sex. The single life was getting old, sometimes lonely and empty. I decided to take a break from any sexual experiences for six months. Arbitrary, I know, but it seemed like the right amount of time to think about my lifestyle. I knew on some level that I was avoiding true intimacy and taking an easier road.

The particularly crazy week mentioned above had included three separate relationships I was juggling: one man just released from jail for assaulting a police officer, another man a police officer and another a married, yet separated, man. They were just like me, seeing other people and no one wanted a commitment. It was just too much for me, and I asked myself what it was I was doing. I was in a blizzard, making decisions without a clear vision. What did I really want in my life as far as relationships?

I have a neat tradition of setting goals for myself every year, although I have slacked the last few years. I have always been a believer in setting personal goals, even if I don't reach them. To me, the importance lies *in the process of setting the goals.* When I think deeply about what I want and clearly identify it, I have a big picture of what is important to me and where I want to go.

Setting goals gives me an idea of what is truly in my heart. What is it that makes me happy? What is it I need to change? What I am striving towards? And, just as important, what is working well? And lastly, what do I want to keep doing?

I strongly believe we all have a purpose here on earth, and God or whoever you believe in has goals and dreams for us. I believe we have to pray to find out what path we should be on for our higher purpose as well. For me, my paths have always seemed to be synchronized; doing social work is God's work and I believe that working in such a field, one has to grow and develop within themselves to be truly effective. Despite making very little money over the years, work is one area of my life that has brought me tremendous satisfaction. I know I have been on the right spiritual path in that area of my life.

In 1988, I set my goals to match some of the changes I wanted to make. I was tired of the partying as it was getting old and I started to find it empty. I wanted something more. I somehow still have the goals I set in 1988 and kept for 1989. I absolutely love looking at this list from time to time; It is in my daily reading book. Some of the goals from that year are relevant to this section, and speak to what was in my heart.

Here goes:

*Things to Keep, Things to Change (1988- 1989)*

- *continue to be honest with myself and others, speaking from my heart, not being afraid to say and feel whatever is there*
- *slow down, relax more, smell the roses, more days like today, more inner peace and strength- keeping my optimism and spirit towards life*
- *exercise more, eat and drink less, lose ten pounds*
- *continue to grow closer to my family-beautiful feeling, to love without judgment, me!*
- *save money- $ 1,000 by end of year*
- *explore leave time options but be flexible, try to realize that I Cannot have it all*

- *search for love that has meaning, depth, trust, intimacy, do not sell self at any cost- be fair to me first, love is out there!*
- *not have as many (or any) one night stands*
- *continue to grow and explore my many wonderful and beautiful friendships*
- *continue to learn and enjoy my job, balancing demands better and worry less*
- *continue to be vulnerable, to enjoy living and to feel all that I can, all is life!!*

I started making some big changes in 1988 and 1989. I ended up meeting a wonderful man in 1989 and we became very serious, fell in love and got married. He is the father to our two children. We started a family very quickly and our relationship lasted about six years. We had some good times and some major struggles, and we co-parented well overall after we broke up and we remain friends today. The greatest gifts in my life *without a doubt* have been my children. I still enjoy being a mother like no other role, and now I am experiencing being a grandmother.

The fact is, we all make choices along the way in blizzard conditions and when we can see more clearly, we try and understand what we did and make changes if necessary. It is very possible to learn from our choices and move forward. Nothing is ever lost, because every experience offers a silver lining that we must look for. It is the silver lining that makes life worthwhile.

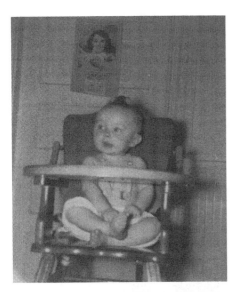

Top left: Kevin as a baby

Top right: Kevin age 8

Bottom: Melissa, Mom, Kevin at age 10

Top: Kevin and Melissa

Bottom left: Mary Riley Mannix

Bottom right: Fred Mannix, Sr.

Top: Kevin and Jeff age 4

Bottom: Kevin and Taylor age 1

Top Right: Kevin speaking at awareness function

Middle: Channel 8 WAGM Presque
Isle News Team 1986

Bottom: WCSH New Center team,
Sharon Rose Vaznis, Lee Nelson,
Kevin. *Photo courtesy of WCSH-6*

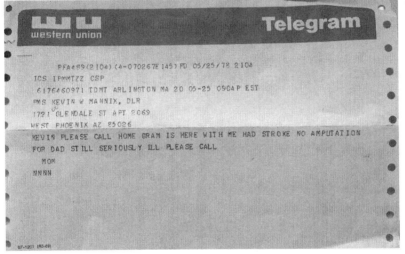

Telegrams from Kevin's mother

Top: Linda's Mom, Anne

Middle: 1961 Family Photo

Bottom left: Linda age 2

Bottom right:

Linda: High School Graduation

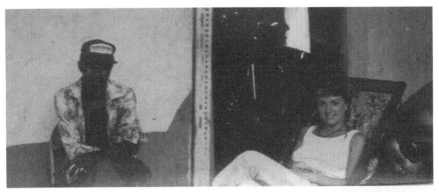

Top: Linda in Africa

Middle: Annah and Linda, pregnant with Emily, 1994

Bottom: Linda with both daughters

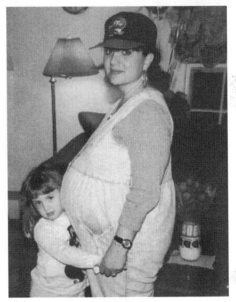

Top: Letters written by Anne when hospitalized

Bottom: Linda's Dad  John and stepmom Carol 2002

Top: Linda with her brothers, Michael, Linda, John and Bobby

Bottom: Kevin and Linda's Wedding with all their children, Emily, Annah, Kevin, Linda, Taylor and Jeff

Left: Kevin and Linda as neighbors

Right: Kevin and Linda today

# 4

# THE STORM BEFORE THE CALM

## *Feeling Out of Control*


*Kevin's Story....*

There are violent storms such as tornados and hurricanes. The storms I am talking about in this chapter are relative to my life before I pursued group therapy and professional guidance.

Both tornados and hurricanes have what are called *damage potential scales.* Tornados are measured on the Fujita Scale from F1 to F5. Hurricanes are measured on the Saffir-Simpson Scale from 1 to 5. I did not have any idea how much I was damaged from my childhood. It is hard to put a number on the experience, but at different times in my life I am sure any number would fit. All I knew was that things felt out of control, and I felt sad and depressed. My self-esteem was at zero on any scale. I had a job, food on the table and a place to live. That part was good but I had no energy for anything else.

In the 80's when I was working in Worcester, Massachusetts, I had no idea where to go for help and was petrified to ask anyone afraid of what they would think of me. I knew my Dad drank, so I found an AA meeting (Alcoholics Anonymous) in Worcester and became friends with Jimmy, who has turned out to be like a brother to me and is my best friend to this day. He and a few other attendees spoke during the meeting. I did not speak, but after the meeting he welcomed me to the group and hoped I would come back. I told him I did not drink and he then informed me that I might want to try the ACOA group, which met on Wednesdays.

Jimmy asked if I would like to go with him, as he was also an adult child of an alcoholic. I have to say, I was stunned by his kindness and honesty to me; a complete stranger. I was scared to say yes but did reluctantly and was relieved to have a label or group of people that knew or understood the feelings I had. The relief did not last long because I was afraid I would be recognized for being on TV or radio. I also had to trust that no one would talk outside a meeting and trust was something I had very little of.

I did decide to go to the ACOA Meeting and again did not speak other than to say my name and that I was not sure this was the right place for me. This triggered the topic for the meeting with everyone telling the group the reason for being there and how it helped them, as well as when it did not work for them.

I was shocked to find how well I related to everyone and had to reluctantly accept the fact that I belonged. I was ashamed, to say the least. Stuck on what do next, I kept going to meetings and began to feel a little better. I heard so much talk about counseling and how it was helping others in the group. At that point, I did not choose to see a professional. The reason? I was feeling better so I thought I had solved most of the problem. Little did I know how small the tip of the iceberg was. I believe I heard this phrase at a meeting: *Stinkin Thinkin.* My thoughts were just that- stinky and off base. Good feelings that came from the meetings only lasted as long as it took the old feelings to creep back in.

When I moved to Presque Isle, meetings were harder to find, but I did go once in a while. In late 1989 when I moved to Portland to work at NEWS CENTER 6, I found more meetings but was really afraid of being recognized and having it get back to my boss or co-workers, so my attendance drizzled. It took me until the late 1990's before I started going back.

It was not about getting up some courage to try but because I was feeling so sad and depressed. I knew it was time to return. Meetings made me feel better, but this time not enough to ignore the fact that I may need more and it was time to start some counseling.

I asked my family doctor to recommend some counselors in the area. She thought a man might work best for me rather than a woman, and I remember being very nervous at the first appointment. He had an office in a big house and gave me a choice of what to sit on; a chair or a pillow on the floor. I became very anxious trying to decide. He noticed that right away and he asked what would be more comfortable for me, so I chose the pillow. The rest of that first session became about choices. How hard it was, and still is once in a while, to make even a simple decision like where to sit. He had a very calming demeanor, was soft spoken, kind and gentle. I saw him twice a week for a month then changed to once a week. I liked him very much and he became someone I felt I could trust. By then we had talked about my family and childhood, and for the first time I was able to admit a few things that I really did not understand or remember. It was too painful for me to acknowledge, but I knew on some level that:

1. Mom had a mental illness and was out of control.

2. Dad was an alcoholic and he was out of control.

3. While I thought I was a controlling person and was in control, it was just the opposite. I was out of control.

I had been deeply affected by the environment I grew up in but was completely unaware that it was the cause of all the bad feelings I had about myself and led me to the choices I made. The thoughts in my head about myself paralyzed me and I was so hurt deep down inside. For me it meant feelings of low self-esteem, depression and not being a loveable person.

I am not a very good handyman around the house. This was embarrassing for me because the perception in our culture that men should know how to fix things around the house and under the hood of a car that. I know some of you would say that there are plenty of *How To* books available that I could have learned from, and while that is true, learning for me was accomplished by watching how something is done, and then doing it over and over until I mastered it. That meant asking for help and I had real trouble doing that.

While I still learn best this way, I have more confidence to pick up a book or read instructions and at least give it a try and not invest so much in the outcome. As you can see, I was very hard on myself; thinking I was a failure because I could not do this. I always felt I had to be *everything* to *everyone*.

My depression caused me to isolate myself and run away from conflict, so issues in my marriages were never resolved. My two boys suffered from this behavior. Not feeling loveable made me terrified about being left by my wives, thinking they would find someone more attractive and smarter than me. This fear made me a people pleaser, clinging to them, which left me with a feeling of frustration underneath the hurt and sadness. I acted all this out with anger. The anger would surface as a protection from feeling the helplessness and hopelessness of the situation I was in at the time. I was grumpy, snappy, defensive and self-absorbed. This is what I learned about myself in the first six months of therapy.

My therapist was ending his practice and suggested a few names for me to contact. For me all the new knowledge meant maybe I could figure out how to make changes on my own, so I stopped therapy, thinking things would be different. Sadly, for ten years I thought I was doing better with everything, but that came crashing down with another divorce and all the old feelings returned. This is sometimes called *hitting bottom.* A five on the Saffir-Simson or Fujita scale for me. I went back to therapy and back to a weekly ACOA meeting, only this time I had a real purpose. I was ready to dig deep within myself and really make changes that would stick, but first I had to admit that my pain growing up was repeated by me in my adult life towards the ones I loved.

A very painful admission that still is very painful even today. I also had to learn about patience and forgiveness in order to move forward. I still struggle, but as you will learn in the next chapter, in my experience there is truth to the saying *no pain, no gain.*

*Linda's Story...*

*Go within every day and find the inner strength so that the world will not blow your candle out.*

Katherine Dunham

It was the mid 90's and I was going through my second divorce. My kids were little, we had a house, and I worked part-time. My marriage was falling apart, even though we went to counseling together and tried so hard. It just wasn't working for many different and valid reasons. Different from my first marriage to my African husband, I was very sad about the marital issues and wished we could have worked it out. We separated and then went through a long divorce process.

These were the years in my life I felt the most out of control. I began to experience unexplained symptoms, what I know now were panic attacks. I had moments in my day where I felt I was going crazy, which made me think I was becoming my mother. These feelings would pass and I would be totally grounded again. I would also draw complete blanks, forget basic things, and had severe anxiety about money, living penny to penny. I wasn't sure what to do about the house. I loved our little home in our safe and secure neighborhood, as I grew up in the same house my entire childhood and I desperately wanted that for my children. As a mother, I did not want to work full time, but knew it was what was best for us financially. It was the hardest time in my life, with so much to think about. Divorce ripped me up, especially with children, a home and a dream that had died. No wonder I was having panic attacks and feeling unglued.

I can remember two times where I had panic attacks that were life changing. One time, I had gone to the credit union to do some banking and was standing in a long line. My anxiety grew during this wait and anxious thoughts were flooding my mind. By the time I got to the teller, I forgot my name, forgot why I was there and I looked at the teller with a blank stare. I quickly left and went to my car where I sat and cried. Thankfully, my girls were not with me. However, next to me was a man working on his car with the hood up. He looked over at me, asked if I was okay, and said, *everything will be ok*. It is a memory I will never forget. My girls and I were big fans of the show *Touched by an Angel* and I later realized that he was probably an angel, sent to give me hope. It warms my heart to think of that as I write.

The second time I had a meaningful panic attack was in Boston. I was attending a conference on mental health and the elderly with a group of people. At that time, I was working in a day treatment program with older adults who were living with severe mental illness, many of whom had been at the state hospital in Maine for years and were adjusting to life in the community. It was an incredible job.

In Boston I had to negotiate the subways alone in the afternoon to get to part two of the conference. Subways cause me great anxiety for some reason. I experienced a major panic attack, got lost and never made it to the second part of the conference. I somehow got myself back to the bus station to head home early. I had to breathe myself out of this panic attack, standing on a toilet seat in this huge Boston bus station, with the stall latch locked so no one would see me in there. I was so scared and embarrassed. I truly felt like I was going crazy that day. I managed to get on a bus and called my therapist to try to see her that night. She had been discouraging me from getting on medicine for anxiety, but my family doctor had been telling me for quite a while she thought I should be on something. My therapist told me I was "tough enough" to work through the anxiety without medications and strongly discouraged a prescription. She would say she wanted me to "feel the feelings" and deal with them without meds. She said the anxiety goes way back to my childhood. But I could not do it anymore. I needed more help. I was a mess and saw my therapist the night I came back from Boston. She thought it was such a "big breakthrough", in that I made it home okay and I reached out to her. I said "great that you think that, but I am going on medicine for anxiety whether you agree or not." She understood, and I went on a small dose of an anxiety med.

I have had my normal share of storms in life, mostly created by my own choices or just life itself. I have felt scared, wondering what I should do next, and I have felt embarrassed by some of my earlier choices, especially in front of my family. I feel like the black sheep at times, as I am the only one in my family divorced, not only once, but twice. However, I believe that everything happens for a reason, whether it is hard or easy, good or bad.

The panic attacks eventually taught me how to work on reducing my anxious thoughts and learn to manage and control them. Every relationship taught me something and added to my life in some way. Even the ones that did not work out taught me life lessons. I jump into situations and then have to figure out how to get out. People have often told me I am afraid of nothing and that is actually not true. I am afraid and have many fears, I just don't dwell on them.

My belief that everything will be okay is more powerful than any fear I feel. I like to challenge myself at times, feel the fear, and do it anyway. I now believe there is nothing wrong with feeling fear or being scared. It is all part of living. I like being vulnerable and verbal with my true feelings. I am always self-examining and thinking about things introspectively. I believe that life truly has ebbs and flows like the ocean, but that most of society is not set up that way. Instead, there is judgment and decisions made about what is okay and what is not. I have learned to go inward. What is my truth? How do I want to live my life? What is non-negotiable and what do I let go? Every person will have different answers, but this is a process that always helps me.

I mentioned a conflict in chapter one, in terms of talking about mental illness, suicide, addiction, abuse, and the darkness of such subjects. So many topics are just so hard to bring out into the light, so hard to start talking about or to even think about. There are many feelings or experiences that can create a deep feeling of shame and take hold on us until we work through it. Some people never do, the storm keeps building inside them. In John Bradshaw's bestselling book, *Healing the Shame that Binds You* he states that,

> *"There are two forms of shame: nourishing shame and toxic life-destroying shame. Toxic shame is an excruciatingly internal experience of unexpected exposure. It is a deep cut felt primarily from the inside. It divides us from ourselves and from others. In toxic shame, we disown ourselves. And this disowning demands a cover-up. Toxic shame parades in many garbs and get-ups. It loves darkness and secretiveness. It is this dark aspect of shame that has evaded our study."*

He goes on to say that *toxic shame ...*

> *"... is a rupture of the self with the self. It is like internal bleeding. Exposure to oneself lies at the heart of toxic shame. A shame-based person will guard against exposing his inner self to others, but more significantly, he will guard against exposing himself to himself."*

Bradshaw also says,

> "To truly be committed to a life of honesty, love and discipline, we must be willing to commit ourselves to reality...(this) requires the willingness and the capacity to suffer continual self-examination...such an ability requires a good relationship with oneself...this is precisely what no-shame based person has...in fact a toxically shamed person has an adversarial relationship with himself".

This book by Bradshaw is amazing in its explanation of how toxic shame develops, and steps for transforming this shame, among many other related chapters. It is a must-read on the topic of shame.

Understanding shame has helped me profoundly. As much as I felt the stigma of my mother's suicide, I did not translate it into toxic shame. I always felt in touch with my inner self, even when I made bad decisions. I have never felt defective as a person, for which I am grateful. That is one storm I do not have to work through.

I did feel the stigma from the outside looking in. I felt shame from the way society looks at suicide. I worried about the judgment of my mother's suicide, and how embarrassed I was about that. I did not know how to bring up the subject. This feels different to me than what Bradshaw describes. I felt some aspects of shame, but did not internalize it to a point where it took over, defining who I was. Maybe this is because I had a clear structure to my life and many positive parenting influences from my dad and stepmom. However, many other people are not so fortunate. In my work, and even with Kevin, the shame itself becomes that person and they do not feel worthwhile and feel they are bleeding internally. I know Kevin still struggles with his core self, with whether or not he is even a good person and a good man. He goes back to that place often, and it is a major struggle in our relation-ship. I feel frustrated and want him to be more confident and unafraid. I want him to believe in himself and feel that mistakes are okay, and to like himself. I struggle with this lack of belief in himself and the effect it has on us. In actuality, underneath that frustration, it breaks my heart.

# 5

# THE EYE OF THE HURRICANE

## *Finding Our Calm Center*

*"As a hurricane moves over us, the winds and rain briefly stop and there is blue sky and sunshine for a short time. This is called the eye of the storm, and then the wind and rain return, slowly subsiding as the storm moves away."*

*Kevin's Story...*

I feel the hurricane quote is a good description of my journey toward recovery. Many rough starts, brief calm and then a downward slide back into turmoil and discomfort about my inner most personal thoughts. It was this cycle that kept repeating over and over. I wanted to reach the calm center and stay there forever.

I wanted to erase the intense feelings of shame, low self-esteem, lack of confidence, fear and anger that have defined me for as long as I can remember. That was the goal when I started my self-journey. This changed along the way, as recovery is truly a journey on a road I will be traveling the rest of my life. In the beginning this was a big disappointment because I wanted to be cured instantly. I did not want to feel like I was defective anymore. I found out after a short time that cure was not the word at all, it was acceptance. I could change some things but some things were part of who I am and will not ever change. I won't lie; I did not accept this right away. At the time I was heading into my forties and I thought, *I am a big boy now, I can change. I can fix this.* Nope, the fixer in me never had any success with that at all. Becoming aware of my pattern of behavior was not enough. In order for me to move forward, I had to accept that I have certain characteristics that will be part of me forever.

For instance: feelings still surface in my marriage about my lack of confidence that I am or could be loveable. Now with awareness and acceptance this feeling doesn't usually feel as strong or last as long. I am still surprised and shocked when that sick feeling in my stomach returns. The one that takes me by surprise.

My conscious self knows that Linda loves me, but I don't trust that when my feelings surface that I am not loveable or worthy. Putting everyone else's feelings ahead of mine always gets me into trouble as well. I still struggle with voicing my honest feelings. Not because I am being dishonest about the feelings I have, it is just that in my mind they hold no value. I am always asking myself, *am I being selfish?*

Needless to say, I struggle to just speak up and trust that my loved ones accept me for who I am. An even harder part for me was and still is asking for and getting forgiveness for the pain that I have caused. I can ask, but it is the feedback that I am worried about. Especially from my sons, which has been so hard to hear because the one thing I know is that I cannot change the past. I have promised myself to be a better dad and husband than the role model I grew up with. I have always been cautious about drinking in fear I could become like my father. I was and have always been a very loyal husband. I have never physically abused my boys or my wives. My downfall was that I was just not emotionally present, I did not know how to be there.

I did not live with Jeff and his mom for long before our divorce, and I moved several times as I was building my broadcast career. I spent very little time with him growing up. When he did visit I devoted all my spare time with him, planning fun times that father and sons do together, but not much of that was nurturing in any way. No talk of feeling, because during that time I quite frankly had no idea how, and it was too uncomfortable to even try. In spite of this, Jeff turned out to be a fine young man, thanks mostly to his mom. He is married to a wonderful woman and is the radio voice for The Portland Pirates of the American Hockey League. I feel his love and forgiveness, but there are times I feel a great loss and sadness for the time we both lost as he was growing up.

When Jeff started working for the Pirates, his mother wanted to come down to Portland to see him. I knew she had been struggling with Alzheimers', and Linda suggested she stay with us, to which I said, "are you nuts"? Linda reminded me that it was more about Jeff than her and I, and I agreed. We invited her to stay, and she was initially supposed to stay for one night. After 3 nights, I decided it was time for her to go. While she was with us, she would come over to the couch and sit next to me. Linda pointed out that with her memory issues, perhaps she still thought we were married. We did have a few good conversations, and were able to forgive each other. I was able to be there for Jeff when she passed away in 2012, and that was probably the best thing I could have done for him.

My younger son Taylor and I still have work to do on our relationship. His mom and I divorced when he was around ten and he spent his childhood living between his mother's home and mine. He was mad at both of us, but only seemed to be mad at the one he was not living with at the time.

Unlike Linda and her ex-spouse, Taylor's mom and I could not get along and unfortunately he was the one who suffered the most. I selfishly focused on my pain and feeling of abandonment and did not deal with how he was feeling, nor did I help him cope with the divorce. It was very painful for him then, and probably most likely still is. In fact, it is still very painful for me.

We spent most of our time together going to Bruins, Celtics and Red Sox games. I took a great interest in his school sports, and he was an exceptional soccer goalie in high school. I made a point to drive him to practice and went to most of his games that my work schedule would allow. I actually thought that was enough. Now I know he really needed more and I just did not have it to give. Past mistakes we both have to live with. I cannot tell you how sad I feel for him and the regrets I have. He was such a great kid, now a great young man, and deserved better. I try not to beat myself up anymore but sometimes when I think about it all, I am so sad at what we both lost and I want to do everything to make up for it now. This is all part of finding that calm center within me and it is not easy work.

I recently had lunch with Taylor, and told him that I was sorry I had neglected him when he was young. Sure, I took him to soccer practices, Red Sox games, etc., but when we got home, I would go upstairs to bed. This left him alone, to get dinner by himself, and created more a rift between us. I apologized to him and said I was very sorry for this He just looked at me and said, "Wow, Dad, that's the first time you said that where I really, truly believe you. That you mean it." He put his arms around me and said, "Thank you, that really means a lot to me". He texted me the next day, saying " I really want to thank you again for your apology, it meant a lot. And I believe you. I also want you to know I appreciate the time we spent together, and I know you love me and I love you". It was so incredibly powerful.

I spent a lot of good times with my boys, and we would have some father/sons conversations, but we were never really close until I started my journey of self-awareness 7 or 8 years ago. The boys have forgiven me; they know it is in the past, and we are moving forward.

At times I feel a great sadness and feel very lonely. I go to a weekly men's group to find the support I need to work through these discouraging feelings. I check in with my counselor from time to time when I feel like I am stuck. I hope this does not sound negative, because for me knowing I need help with this and reaching out for it is an uplifting, positive course of action. I want to keep moving forward with my recovery and not go back to those darker times and emotional bad habits.

When I remember how bad I felt, it reminds me how much I do want to stay focused in the present. A better place; not perfect, but better, as I no longer suffer in silence with these feelings. I feel frustrated sometimes that I struggle, but no shame. While this process works well for me, I remind anyone reading this that your journey may be totally different, but worth the investment. I am not endorsing any particular type of therapy as an answer. I only wish to offer a little hope that if we can find the courage to take a look at what is at the root of our struggle, our journey will be underway and we can take charge and steer it in whatever direction works for us.

*Linda's Story...*

*Emancipate yourselves from mental slavery, none but ourselves can free our minds.*

Bob Marley

The eye of the hurricane sounds so peaceful. It is the before and after times that are scary and dangerous. Like Kevin, finding my calm center has been an ongoing journey. I think it always works that way. Being honest about our struggles and not being afraid to look at our issues is how we get there. I was only really able to understand my mother's suicide and the effect it had on me after I went to counseling for the first time in my twenties.

Although I had functioned well and achieved my goals, I had an unresolved part that affected me every day. This part caused me anxiety and angst. One of my favorite anonymous quotes says *It is what we don't look at that rules us.* This was so true for me. I always felt anxiety and angst around the topic of suicide, and had no idea how that was ever going to change. I even felt anxiety around the topic of mothers. I did not know how much this unresolved part of my life was truly affecting me.

As I mentioned in Chapter 3, I had come home from Africa with a man and had ninety days to get married. I was not ready for marriage, let alone being married to a man that was totally new to this country. We did get married but it was not working for me after a short while. A dear friend of mine told me I needed help in sorting out my struggles and I should try counseling. She recommended someone, and I called and made an appointment. I was very scared, as I had no idea what counseling would be like, let alone what I would end up feeling. I was not sure if it would be worse to open up about my past and how it affected me. Worried about what she would ask me, and if she thought I was crazy,

I was actually very afraid of this whole process but thought I would try it.

Counseling has helped me make sense of my life more than anything else has. It has helped me understand what it is I feel and why. Counseling gave a name to my feelings that were so mysterious. The first time, I went to this incredible women who listened to my current situation and then asked about my childhood. She asked if I had ever sorted out my childhood issues, to which I replied *no* and cried. It was our very first session. She did not have any tissues handy, so she ran upstairs and came down with a roll of toilet paper. I knew then she was the one for me. We talked about my childhood, how childhood forms our lives, and what my current situation had to do with my childhood and how that formed who I had become. She was very nonjudgmental and very nontraditional, a great combination for me. She did not think I was crazy at all, and said my situation was very normal, understandable, and I would start to see what she meant after we worked together awhile. I felt very comfortable this first session, and could not wait to go back.

I want to point out that I am not writing this to push counseling. It happened to help me several times in my life, but that is my experience. I know other people who feel it has not been helpful for them. I am hoping that readers find what works for them if they have a story of shame to work through, whatever that might be. The goal of our book is to encourage people to reach out, feel less embarrassed by their struggles, and find someone or something to help them sort out their feelings and move forward.

I was twenty-six when I first started talking about my mother's suicide to a professional. Very few people in my life knew about my mother, as it was so hard for me to talk about. I am very thankful I had a wonderful counselor who I clicked with on every level and felt safe to open up. Having a person you feel safe with is so important. I cried about the pain of my loss and how I wished my mother was still alive. The counselor told me that was okay to feel and to mourn the relationship that I never had with her. Somehow I needed to hear that it was okay to feel what I was experiencing, even though I knew it intellectually. We worked on this issue for a while then moved on to other feelings from childhood. She helped me understand the reason behind some of my choices, or why I would feel something intuitively and not always listen. She helped me see why casual relationships, where I did not get too emotionally attached, were easier for me. She said my independent and impulsive nature was both a blessing and a safety net. As I said in Chapter 3, I am quite certain that it was comfortable to be carefree with men because it was easier than being committed. Deep down I was very afraid of being stuck in a commitment and of abandonment, as I learned in counseling. She helped me see the things that can stifle me, such as being too open or too impulsive or even too kind. I will forever be grateful to this woman who worked with me for two years and helped me make sense of my world as a child. I am not sure where I would be today if I did not get great professional support to learn about myself and begin to weave my mother's suicide into my life story. I could finally say those words out loud without hiding under a rock.

As I mentioned before, my late twenties were very formative years. I worked in a very tough job as a child protective worker and made some great leaps as far as understanding myself. I still made choices that were not the smartest, but with a deeper understanding and the ability to reflect. I was growing as a person and felt a little better about the topic of suicide and mothers, as it now had an open place in my life story with a deeper understanding and the ability to reflect.

Over the years I have been involved in individual therapy, marriage counseling, group therapy, Al-Anon meetings and have been to a few retreats. I have gone years without doing any formal work on myself. I have always been a deep thinker, going inward. I like to sit quietly and meditate. I like to light a candle and breathe softly, listening to my breath go in and out. I like to sit in nature and be calm and centered with daily spiritual readings. I like watching movies or reading stories that move me, ones that make me feel something deeply. It could be a super funny movie that makes me laugh until I cry or one that makes me sit in my seat for an hour after, unable to move. It has been good to go in and out of getting professional help, as I could live what I learned, although sometimes I take one step forward, two steps back. Life has truly been that way for me. Now I recognize when I need to get more help to work through something and get back in balance. Again, I share my healing journey only as it has been for me. Every person has their own path, one that works for them and what they carry around. Our personal healing journeys need to be individualized and very meaningful to each of us.

The second time I did individual counseling was when I was in my mid to late thirties going through my second divorce. This was the hardest time of my life. Once again I had a wonderful counselor who was life-changing. She was very different than the first counselor I had ten years earlier, as she was very tough on me and less into feelings. She would listen to my feelings, acknowledge them, and then want to make an action plan to move forward. We worked on the art of letting go and the importance of being more discriminatory while dating. Now, that is an interesting story. The counselor felt that I was not able to differentiate between a good man who I might be attracted to in many ways and a man that I was actually compatible with. I have never really looked at relationships solely in terms of compatibility. She tried to help me see that a good man doesn't necessarily equal a good partner. Some of you might be asking if I am clueless, but that is where I was in my life. I always thought if you had enough in common then you could work out the rest. She really set me straight on that.

My counselor had me write a personal ad with the idea of talking with men over the phone to start to learn about compatibility. She did not want me to necessarily meet the man in person, but try and talk about important things on the phone and filter out the men I was not compatible with. I was looking for compatibility in communication style, values, interests, and life goals, to mention a few. Sometimes it was very obvious and other times not. She asked me to meet the men I wanted to meet in public places only, as I had not been very careful in the past. I ended up violating the agreement on the first date. I met a man at a coffee shop and ended up going to his house, which happened to be on the ocean, which is my downfall. We had a great time, but I immediately realized it was the old me. I was doing exactly what I was used to doing.

At my next counseling session, I was honest and told her what I did. She agreed it was not the plan, but was very pleased that I immediately saw where I had gone wrong. Another man I met was absolutely gorgeous and I wanted so badly to go home with him. But during our date he drank many non-alcoholic beers and told me he was just out of rehab, still married and in some legal trouble. He walked me to my car and the logical side of my brain actually kicked in and I knew he was not right for me. I could tell he was a good man but not in a good place at this time in his life. I thanked him for the date and told him we were in very different places in life. I wished him the best as he sorted out his life and we kissed briefly. I drove off and felt the tremendous power of making a smart choice. To some, this is probably a no-brainer. For me, it was a life-changing moment that I will never forget. It began a new journey of being more careful and realizing I had personal power to choose relationships. I had several similar dates and began to sincerely understand the art of discernment in dating.

Another profound lesson learned from this round of counseling had to do with my children. I realized that they would be okay through the divorce if their dad and I took care of ourselves. If we were okay, they would be okay. We eventually were able to come together and co-parent pretty well. Some years we cele-brated holidays together and it was wonderful, and still do gather together at times. My counselor left me with another big piece of wisdom. During our sessions, she learned that I was a very careful and safety-oriented mother. She said I took better care of my girls than I did of myself. She encouraged me to think of them when I was making a big decision, ask what I would tell my girls about this and that would give me the answer I needed. That wisdom has come in handy many times as my innate sense of safety for them is stronger than my innate sense of safety for myself. This may be true for many other women as well.

# 6

# RIDING THE JETSTREAM

## *Learning to Live with the Flow*

*Jet streams are the major means of transport for weather systems.*

*Kevin's Story...*

In our neck of the woods the jet stream flows west to east. It pushes high and low pressure systems. Highs usually mean good weather with a significant amount of sun and little or no wind. Low pressure usually means bad weather with clouds, snow, rain, thunder and lightning that can grow into tornados and wind that can grow to hurricane strength.

Much like our lives, we have happy, quiet times and periods of turmoil, pain and sadness. Learning to accept both continues to be a struggle from time to time, even after fifteen years of dedicated difficult work that has challenged me to visit memories I haven't dared to before. I now have a  better understanding of myself and feel more confident, accepting myself for who I am and the choices I have made. I know I am a good person.

I have always enjoyed the growth and support of viewers watching *The Morning Report* as part of a great team in front of and behind the camera, but that was my job. However, over the years my focus has been to build a more positive, stronger relationship with my sons.

Being alone gave me the opportunity to get comfortable with myself and continue to look at times of low self-esteem and sadness that would still come up from time to time. It began to feel manageable. It gave me that false sense of having it all figured out. That changed one Friday in September, six years ago in 2009.

I was driving home from work that morning and was going to stop for some milk, but thought I would go home and change first. A red light not only changed my mind, it changed my life. I was stopped in front of the store, so I decided that I might as well get the milk now. In the store, I ran into an old friend from the neighborhood where Linda and I lived years ago. He asked me to go to the Portland High School football game with him that night. Friday night was not my favorite night to go out after a long week of getting up at 2 AM, but I really thought it would be fun to get out, so I accepted the invitation.

I did not pay much attention when this woman sat down beside me, but at a second glance, I saw it was Linda. It had been 10 years since I last saw her. Her daughter was a cheerleader and we talked for a while about the game and caught up, then she returned to her seat. I remember thinking that she had such happy positive energy but did not remember her being so cute and attractive. She knew I worked at Channel 6, so she called the weather department and left a message for me. We all used the same voice mail, so I never checked it. We ran into each other the following week at another Portland High School game and she told me I never called her back. We swapped numbers, and I called her a few days later to make sure we did not miss each other. We went on a date to the Top of the East, a restaurant on the top of the Eastland Hotel in Portland. I told her my story and I am still surprised to this day that she did not run away as fast as she could. However, something clicked for both of us and we kept seeing each other. That is when I discovered I still had so much work to do on building healthy relationships and how I saw myself in being part of one. It started yet another new journey of dealing with extreme highs and lows and learning to live with that flow I so desperately wanted.

As we continued dating, I found my old role in relationships was still alive and well, much to my surprise. After all, being loving, kind, truly committed and wanting to be helpful in a relationship is who I am. The problem arises when I overdo it. I get so busy trying to be helpful, only to realize later it was the old need to be seen as loveable. Once again, I found it hard to listen. I did not hear Linda, who, by the way, is a very independent person, say she needed space or likes to do things on her own. In my mind I was thinking *what a great guy I am to help out.* She is thinking *what a needy pain in the ass you are.*

The point I kept missing is that a true loving relationship is about listening. In fact, any relationship works best when you can listen, which is an extremely hard skill for a guy who grew up needing to think ahead all the time to feel safe. The wonderful thing here is that I do feel safe and loved by Linda. I am now on the heels of a very active jet stream with strong highs and lows for the past five years.

Linda wanted to end the relationship more than once when we were dating. She felt smothered. I was feeling loved, but my fear of abandonment would not allow me to feel secure. *She would see my struggles and leave*, I thought. I was very clingy because of that fear. The funny thing was that she was telling me what bothered her and I could not hear it. I tended to filter what I heard and my mind would start working on a solution as soon as she would start to talk, and she would feel ignored. She just wanted to share feelings and not have me ready to jump on my white horse and save her. We worked very hard on our issues and decided to get married about a year and a half after reconnecting.

The hardest part in the beginning was blending our families. Our work schedules turned out to be a problem for me, as I would get up at 2 AM five days a week and work until 11 AM, while Linda's schedule was more 9 to 5. I had the house to myself to unwind, do chores and prepare dinner. When Linda got home it did not dawn on me that she might need some space and time to unwind like I did in the morning. I was happy to see her and wanted to interact right away. She could not and I did not get it. I enjoyed the opportunity to come home to an empty house. Not considering her needs, or even extending the same process to her, left me feeling rejected. No matter how much Linda said she cared or loved me, the minute it felt like she needed space, it triggered the feeling I was not good enough and that it was only a matter of time before she would leave. The thought I was pushing her away never entered my mind. We also had many good times in between my bouts with doubt. I did not ignore her on purpose, it was just so hard for me to accept that I was in a very loving relationship where my needs were being heard. While I was busy protecting myself I did not hear what Linda was needing from me.

The old fears resurfaced and the struggles of how I was feeling about any given situation blocked me from seeing how and what Linda was feeling or saying. I did not see I was needlessly self sabotaging the relationship and rocking the boat.

Linda would always ask me where I was in the boat. It took a six month separation for me to be able to answer her. When Linda first moved out I was devastated and filled with anger. I thought I had done my best, so why would she leave? Again at that point

94

I could not see the pain and frustration she was feeling. I thought this was the beginning of the end and there was no going back. In hindsight it was good to take a break. Linda really needed one, and in the end it was good for me as well. We continued to see each other and talk because we knew we still cared and loved one another.

I slowly started to understand that I was not listening to what Linda was feeling at all. If I had really listened to her side without judgment, all my anxiety would not have arisen and we probably would not have needed a separation. Our honest talks made me realize how sad and hurt Linda was by my silence, reluctance to take charge and lack of understanding of her feelings. So I saddled up my horse and headed back to therapy. This time the goal was to figure out what I was missing and the tools I needed to move forward.

This wonderful relationship with a fantastic lady who I love dearly had brought me back to a place that I thought I had left behind. It was a big lesson learned, but more importantly I had to forgive myself for the unintentional pain I had caused Linda. I had to make amends with Linda and build back her trust in me. It was a slow and sometimes painful process but I loved her so much. The love I felt for her was not desperate in any way, it was different than my other relationships. It had a peacefulness that came from a true feeling that my love for her was reciprocated unconditionally. We truly had a future together and since we got back together our relationship has been doing quite well. Not perfect, but what relationship really is? We are evolving together, growing as a couple. Now our struggles show that there is a lesson to learn and room for growth. I do feel loved, really loved.

Earlier in this chapter I touched on how part of my new-found confidence came from the success at my job. That confidence was shattered September, 2014. The month that contract talks on a new deal with NEWS CENTER were to begin. I was looking for a one or two-year deal, and was shocked to learn that the company did not want to give me another contract. Once the old one expired in December 2014, I was done. My replacement had already been hired and the company wanted me off the morning show in October. It was ironic that this decision came just a couple of weeks before the station and I received multiple awards from The Maine Association of Broadcasters for my series *Kevin's Story,* which of course inspired Linda and myself to write this book.

Hearing this news four or five years ago would most likely have sent me over the edge and into a rage of rejection. Instead I calmly expressed my shock, dismay and disappointment to the news director. My first thought was that I had been with WCSH for twenty-five years and was a loyal employee, no one ever told me I was not. I expressed my sadness that this was not considered nor was my popularity with the audience. I also talked about the MAB awards and the other awards and honors Linda and I had recently received.

The series has led to more than usual personal appearance requests. Right around contract renewal time I was in Augusta for a walk-a thon, hosted the Battle of the Bands for Charity in Bangor, judged lobster recipes for charity in Rockland and I was at a church group in North Windham. The common theme from each organizer was that my on-air promotion and my participation the day of the event was a great help towards their fund raising goals. Viewers of all ages spoke to me at these appearances and expressed their appreciation for my forecasting, as well as how much fun they have had watching me every morning.

I pointed this out to the news director and asked how this led to their decision. His response was that he thought I would be busy writing the book and not want to be working full time any more. My response was that I wish I had been consulted and he not just assume my future plans. I want to point out that in the television industry, if the station wants you out, your contract is either bought out or not renewed. You get a bit of time to clean out your desk, turn in your key and get escorted out the door. Sometimes without a chance to say goodbye to colleagues and friends you worked with for years. It can be a very cold ending without explanation.

I am very thankful they did not choose that route for me and respected my years of service. I was able to negotiate a short term contract for an additional two months, which is rare. With that said, it still was a very tough time, not only for me but for my replacement. We already had a long term friendship and professional relationship, and we were both put in an awkward position. Being the professionals that we are, we were able to maintain our friendship as he reached out to me right at the beginning, which meant a lot to me. I was able to pick the date of my last *Morning Report* and had a week long sendoff that was both fun and bittersweet at the same time.

I have to say, it was so much fun reminiscing the many funny moments on The Morning Report. I was also sad, because I still feel so much excitement when it comes to forecasting the weather and that role was being diminished so quickly.

I heard from hundreds of viewers that week; thanking and telling me how much they would miss me and what I meant to them. Regardless of all the viewer's words, you can guess what

I felt for the next five months. I felt rejected for not being wanted anymore and felt like the twenty-five years of hard work meant nothing. I reached out to other stations but no one was hiring. I started to look at public relations jobs and tried to think about what else I could do.

Linda kept saying I had so much value with my face and name recognition but my heart was not in it. I was in the frame of mind that I once again had no value. No one wants an older me. Everyone was looking for the younger face. I was angry about what had happened, and working the noontime show felt like a demotion. I was worried about money and how we would get by. I was so afraid that if I could not find something else to do, Linda would surely leave me. Yes, I was throwing a huge pity party for myself. I was also scared about what would happen in two months, when our initial agreement ended. It would either be another extension or the end of the road.

Looking ahead, I knew I was in trouble, so I got our finances in order with help from my brother-in-law, who knows far more about retirement investments than I do. It was really hard to admit that to him but he was incredibly helpful.

Another thing I learned was that it is okay to admit that I don't know everything. I started discussions with my news director about working with him and the station on promotions and marketing for this book. His response was a strong commitment of an open dialogue around shame and stigma issues and we have had great conversations about how to move forward.

That is when I started to feel like I was letting go of that job and was looking forward to finishing the book and heading down a new, unknown, and exciting path. I reached out to friends and colleagues, doing some self promotion of the Kevin Mannix brand to reduce my anxiety a little. The anxiety that was left was focused on my ability to believe in myself and the concept of this book. The more positive responses I received, the more my confidence grew and doors opened. During my *pity party,* Linda was very supportive of this process to a point. She knew I needed a dose of tough love and gave me a kick in the butt to get me back on track. When she was finished talking, I knew I was loved but needed to get moving forward. She wanted me to see my value the way she saw me and put myself out there in a positive way. I knew she was not going anywhere and that we would face the future as a couple, riding the roller coaster of ups and downs together, hand in hand.

My last full time broadcast was February 27th 2015. I announced it Tuesday of that week on social media. The station and I agreed to call it a sort of semi-retirement: full retirement from the day to day broadcasts with some per diem gigs covering vacations.

I learned some really positive things through this process. Once again hundreds of comments poured in, and this time I allowed myself to feel and believe in the outpouring of love and appreciation sent my way by family, loyal fans and colleagues. It was powerful to take it in when you let it. It allowed me to think of those twenty-five years as meaningful and a blessing. That job allowed me to come into so many homes and become a true friend to viewers all those years. I met so many wonderful people at appearances; some that have become close friends. Some solid friendships also developed with the many great and talented people I worked with in front of, and behind the camera at NEWS CENTER. They are the parts of that job I will miss the most.

I have said before how much I love forecasting the weather, so much so that I do it every day for work or play. Another thing I have realized is that there were many things I did in my job that

I just did not feel comfortable with anymore, and it felt good to let them go.

I have heard from viewers over and over again that my courage to go public with my shame issues meant so much to them. Feeling uncomfortable in my job and the encouragement I received allowed me to deeply feel that it was time to leave television fulltime. I could let go and feel comfortable and excited about my new career. My focus would now shift to a new passion. I walked off of the set and into a new world where I know Linda and I will make a positive difference, and I could not feel any more excited about our journey.

Do I have regrets? You bet I do. If I could do a lot of things over, I would. All I can do is go forward from here; I am still working on my relationship with my boys, which gets better every day. I still have my anxiety- It is like a trick knee. I never know when It is going to rear up, or when something may trigger it and it grabs me by the throat. But through counseling I have acquired the necessary tools to deal with it, and am much better equipped to handle what comes my way.

It does get easier.

*Linda's Story...*

*It takes courage to grow up and turn out to be who you really are.*

E.E. Cummings

I have looked forward to writing this chapter for this entire time. This is the chapter that I feel brings all the hard work we have done in self discovery into action. Life happens and as adults we can decide how we will handle it. Like the jet stream, life itself transports us through many different experiences and challenges. It is within our control as adults to manage those systems, accepting the ups and downs of whatever comes our way and ride out the storms. Granted there are many events that seem unbearable and very painful, such as the death of a loved one, but I am talking about the day to day challenges that we all face. A big part of this chapter is about embracing our personal challenges, accepting the truth that exists and learning to live fully within that truth.

Nothing hits home more in terms of acceptance than being a single parent. This section is a big shout-out to all the single parents. I was a single parent for fifteen years, and the girls saw their father every week, as he was involved and very loving. However, the day-to-day was me and my girls, learning to live fully, happily, and without shame.

My girls were young when their dad and I separated. At one and five years old, it was a major adjustment for them. I had to work full time again, something I desperately wanted to avoid. I remember one night when my older daughter and I were doing the dishes I mentioned that I had to work full time again and I started crying. She turned to me and said, "Mom, It is going to be fine. We'll be okay!" It struck me that she intuitively knew, at her young age, that we would be okay.

In the beginning, there were many times I felt alone and sometimes shameful of being a single parent. One time I was at the girls' school and my daughter was being presented with an award. As happy and proud as I was, I felt alone. There was no one to turn to that would feel as proud as her own parent did. This type of experience happened a few times, where I felt proud but somehow shamed. Then something clicked for me. I did not want to miss out on the proud moments due to being embarrassed for being alone. I was compromising the joy. I thought to myself that I am here, alone and so what. I was focusing on the wrong thing, because my children were more than thriving and doing great. I was feeling alone as a parent, not fully enjoying the moments that they were experiencing. So what if I was a single parent? I lived in a neighborhood with many intact families so I felt like a fish out of water at times. Again, so what? Why did I feel shameful? I started to understand the need to embrace my life as it was, and enjoy my children and all their adventures and challenges. The reality is that single parenting is probably the hardest thing I have ever done, yet the most joyful and rewarding. The experience of working through these initial feelings and getting to be a strong and very competent family unit was extremely fulfilling.

I grew in confidence during this period of my life. My struggles were still there, but my focus was my children and providing them a secure and loving home. I enjoyed that job more than words could ever express, and I still love being a mother, more than anything. I learned about unconditional love, pure joy and sheer determination. I felt a commitment to something so important and rewarding. That doesn't mean it was easy or something I would choose in an ideal world. Sharing day-to-day parenting with someone would have been the best, but that did not work out, so this was the next best option. I was still the same person, with the same dreams for myself and my children. I learned how to adjust to this jet stream; how to modify and compromise my lifestyle. I had little extra money and often fell short for even basic needs. I will be the first to say that money struggles are very, very stressful and I am sure many people would agree with me. Money struggles can keep you up at night and cause much anxiety. I often had less than zero dollars to my name and lived paycheck to paycheck, yet we always managed and had fun with what we did have. How about macaroni and cheese on a blanket in the living room, pretending we are on a picnic in the dead of winter? Or going to the beach at night with peanut butter and jelly sandwiches and a Frisbee. There was no television during dinner and no TV in anyone's bedroom. I think that helped us bond more and come up with some crazy times.

Just sitting in the living room on many nights listening to my children, talking and laughing, produced some wonderful memories. Creativity soars when money is tight and love is great. This period of my life was the strongest and most meaningful time, as my priority and commitment was crystal clear and very rewarding. Part of this stems from not having my biological mom growing up. I wanted nothing more than to be a great mom and to be there for my girls. It is another example of how a hardship can be a blessing in disguise. It wasn't always easy during the teen years, but we made it through.

I had to learn some more tough personal lessons in this period of time as well. I could speak my mind clearly and firmly, especially if on behalf of my girls. However, it was still very hard and humbling for me to ask for help. That can be a very tough thing for someone who is very independent.

One lesson I learned was on a Christmas afternoon when I was stranded at the movies. It was the first Christmas I was alone, as I had the girls in the morning and their dad had them in the afternoon. I treated myself to a movie to stay occupied and to relax. When I got out and went to start my car, it was dead. Nothing. I felt so alone in the middle of a huge parking lot. My family was all out of state and, although I had a lot of friends, I did not want to impose on anyone on Christmas day. I did not have AAA at the time, and did not know what to do. I went through the list of people nearby in my head and just could not bring myself to call. So I called a cab and had to pay in change. It was a horrible experience and forced me to once again work on my stubborn independent streak. Later, I asked some of my good friends and neighbors if I could call them, anytime, and without hesitation they all responded with "Are you crazy? Of course you can!" I somehow needed to make sure it was okay and then I felt more comfortable asking. It was a worthwhile lesson to learn.

Filing bankruptcy was another big challenge of my jet stream. After my divorce, the debt was divided and we each paid our portion. However, that changed after a year or so and all the debt came to me. A lawyer mentioned bankruptcy as an option, as the debt was overwhelming for my small salary. I cried for days about this dilemma. I was raised to be responsible and to take care of my business, so filing bankruptcy never seemed like an option. That would go against my upbringing and everything I knew about being accountable. However, as the days went on and I had to make a decision, I started to look past the shame of bankruptcy. If I did not file, I would have to work another job, being away from my girls even more. It would take years and years to pay and I would struggle financially even more than I was already. Again, the facts helped me combat the feelings of shame. Even though this choice was very different than how I was raised, I was leaning towards it as a way to stay grounded as a mother and as a worker. I had to slowly learn to accept bankruptcy as the best option under the circumstances, understand the reasons why I was doing it, what my choices were and live with the embarrassment I felt in bankruptcy court. It was awful and demeaning. In time, I knew it was the best choice I could have made. I learned to not let it define me and I had a little quote on my fridge that spoke to me: *You are more than your credit score.* I am not sure where the quote came from, but that little sign helped me more than you'll know. I share this experience for all those out there struggling with financial woes. I am not endorsing bankruptcy by any means, but instead sharing my struggle around shame with a financial dilemma that was very hard.

One of the greatest blessings I did have in this period of my life as a single mom was my family. My brothers each helped me out occasionally, either with a large bill or sending me money for a trip. They all did so without any pressure or any feelings of blame. They knew I worked hard and just did not make enough money. I appreciated that so much. One of my brothers would visit and leave money in my room with a note: *use this for fun only...not for bills.*

My parents would load me up with extra stuff they got from their buy 1 get 2 bargains, and bring other items up from Connecticut when they'd visit. I had a little pantry in the basement that I called *the love pantry,* because I felt loved and cared for whenever I went downstairs to get something. Those simple gifts meant so much to me during a very hard financial time.

As I've mentioned before, I am not one to regret my decisions. Even if something turns out hard, it still happened for a reason. However, I do have one big regret that I still think about. That regret is selling my sweet little home. We had so much fun and great parties in our little home and yard, including a live petting zoo for two birthday parties. I kept up with being a home owner alone for many years, but had a hard time affording the never ending cost. My dad taught us to take care of what we had and the house needed some work. This reality bothered me, as I wanted to take care of it but had no money or time to do so. I tried to put it on the market two times before I actually followed through. I thought selling it would free up money, allow me and my girls to travel, have more freedom and I would have less household maintenance and responsibilities. It was the worst decision, as renting always became problematic and I greatly missed the freedom and stability of a private home. The only good thing to come of it was some fun trips for me and the girls, as I love to travel and wanted them to get the travel bug as well.

We went to NYC, Florida and an overnight cruise on the Scotia Prince. I also became a reunification foster parent during this period of time, which I did for three years. After those three years and a few very difficult situations, I decided to let go of this role. I felt I was not taking care of my own children well enough as I was still a single parent and had a hard time managing all the demands. That was an extremely difficult and painful decision that took me a while to work through.

I want to share a very positive jet stream moment when I was in my late twenties. As previously mentioned, my stepmom and I had our share of struggles during my childhood. She had a very rough start herself, went into the convent and then married my dad who had three motherless children. She was only in her late twenties when she married my dad, and had her hands full. My dad took a backseat and let her take charge of the household. This led to many conflicts and misunderstandings, especially with me, the only girl. However, we all got through it and life went on. My stepmom ended up going to counseling years later and learned some things about herself. She looked back at how she had raised us and wanted to explain some things and apologize to each of us. This was an amazing gift. She talked with each of us and said she was sorry for how tough she was on us and that she was only trying to do her best. She shared much more about her childhood and it helped me understand her. This was a life-changing moment as I was able to accept her apology and realize she did not hate me or purposely be so hard on me as a child. I will forever be grateful for her, as well as the gift of allowing us to remember my mom, as I spoke of earlier. These two gifts changed the direction of my life in a positive way.

As I have said throughout this book, the most important thing in my life is to be true to myself. I even have *Be True to You* as my license plate. As for the jet stream, staying connected to myself and thinking things through calmly and methodically, without anxiety and angst, is key. Life is a constant flow of ups and downs with big and little swoops, and each flow a little different than the last. I have loved my life of flows, with all the ups and downs, pains and joys that it brings with it. Each experience or system is a chance to feel alive, to embrace my challenges in new ways and to love those around me even more fully. My all-time favorite daily reading book, *Simple Abundance - A Daybook of Comfort and Joy* by Sarah Ban Breathnach, sums this up with a quote by Katherine Sharp on February 24: *Sometime in your life you will go on a journey. It will be the longest journey you have ever taken. It is the journey to find yourself.* Finding yourself is key to managing the jet streams of life. Without our own compass, without knowing what it is we need and want, we are lost, victims to the swirling winds around us. Take the winds that come your way, all the light breezes and all the strong gusts, and know that weaving them all together is *your very own beautiful tapestry to love and accept.*

# 7

## Our Extended Outlook

### *Sunnier Skies Ahead*

*An extended outlook is a prediction of future weather based on the analysis of available and pertinent weather data coming from many different sources.*

*Our Story...*

As in a weather forecast, many various data collection sources are used to make the most accurate prediction. In blending our voices, sharing some relevant data, and looking ahead, we want the message of this book to be crystal clear to others that there is hope, help and ways to step out of the storm and into a brighter sky.

Writing this book together has also helped us reflect on our marriage. Over the past five years as a couple, we have had our share of struggles and challenges. Just coming together as two very different people with years of our own baggage has been a learning experience. We have laughed, cried, talked and learned so much about each other and what is really important to the other person. We've had to learn patience with the other's struggles in order to forge an understanding. Continuing to grow as a couple is important to us, as we value our deep connection and commitment. This is new territory for both of us. It is also new territory to really see the gifts the other person brings to the marriage.

As much as differences can bring conflicts, we have learned that they can also bring stability. In our relationship, Kevin's strong belief in commitment helped me take marriage more seriously. Linda is talking more now that I have become a better listener. We have learned to be really honest about our feelings and things that are difficult about the other person. This is leading to more deeply rooted feelings of love and security in our marriage. The work is not easy, and is ongoing. However, the results are like a refreshing summer breeze, peaceful and flowing. Our relationship works because of the ups and downs, then working things out, and becoming stronger.

As we move forward, we want to share that not every individual has a story of deep shame they carry around. We all experience shame in our lives to some extent or another; which is normal. This book has been about the toxic shame discussed in an earlier chapter, the shame that is a deep cut, felt primarily from the inside. The type of shame that causes long term unhappiness, discomfort, confusion and can even paralyze you emotionally. We have shared our own stories of shame and stigma and how that impacted us in this book. Our biggest hope in sharing is that our reader can find the courage to look inward to see if you have a shame story that you have internalized. Is it time to tell your story? Is it time to peek through the blinds to see the sunlight? It is exhausting and lonely to carry the silent burden of shame. Of course not everyone has a heavy burden, but if you do or know someone that does, we hope this book can help with the first step of opening up and sharing your story with a person you trust.

We heard from many viewers after the airing of *Kevin's Story* who thanked us for sharing our struggles. Specifically, many wrote that they decided to seek help after feeling encouraged by the story; several even saying the series had literally saved their lives. We are still very thankful that the series had such impact and now hope the book will do the same.

We want to reiterate some of the main points from our experiences. They are just our thoughts that we want to share with you in hopes our journey will help or inspire you. We are not experts and are not diagnosing or evaluating others. We are people sharing our personal struggles, stumbles and successes. Your journey will be your own unique combination of what works for you. Here's our list of what we feel worked best for us and what we learned in the process. As they say in AA (Alcoholic Anonymous), *take what you like and leave the rest.*

- Without a doubt, taking that first step towards change was a scary one for us.

- We learned there is no magic cure for mental health issues, it is an ongoing journey.

- It takes courage to dig deep, discover and recover.

- It is our responsibility as adults to get the help we need to be healthier; we are not victims.

- We learned that progress can be slow, it can be two steps forward, one step back and it can ebb and flow like the ocean tides but there is general forward movement that offers hope.

- We found relief in understanding why it is we struggle, and labeling or naming our feelings.

- We slowly learned to embrace our struggles and accept our truths.

- We learned we are not alone, that others have experienced similar situations and have similar feelings.

- We learned there is help out there; both professional and non- professional, we just had to find it and to ask for help.

- We remember and believe the saying; *we are the heroes of our own story.*

Many good organizations and individuals have tackled this subject of shame and stigma. There are several books and articles written on its power. It is still hard to talk about things that you cannot see or don't understand. You cannot touch depression, PTSD or anxiety. However, they are as real as a broken leg, cancer, or heart disease. Yet most people Cannot openly say they have clinical depression, or suffer from panic attacks as openly as they could say they just had heart surgery. Although the stigma of having a mental illness may be less today than it was when we were growing up, it still exists.

The Center for Disease Control identifies mental health as *a state of well-being in which the individual realizes his or her own abilities, can cope with the normal stresses of life, can work productively and fruitfully, and is able to make a contribution to his or her community.*
The following are some statistics from the Centers for Disease Control and Prevention, last updated October 2013:

- *CDC estimated that only about 17% of U.S adults are considered to be in a state of optimal mental health. There is emerging evidence that positive mental health is associated with improved health outcomes.*

- *Depression is the most common type of mental illness, affecting more than 26% of the U.S. adult population.*
- *It has been estimated that by the year 2020, depression will be the second leading cause of disability throughout the world, trailing only ischemic heart disease.*

Healthline News published the following information written by Brian Krans and published March 2, 2014:

- *Experts estimate that one in four people have treatable mental or emotional difficulties, but up to 75 percent of Americans and Europeans don't seek the help they need.*
- *A recent study in The Journal of Psychological Medicine shows that the stigma associated with mental illness is still a major barrier to seeking treatment.*
- *Researchers at the Institute of Psychiatry, London examined data from 144 studies, which included over 90,000 participants from across the globe. They found that the stigma of mental illness remains one of the top reasons people choose to forego care.*

The National Institute of Mental Health (NIMH) reports the following:

- *40 to 50 percent of all people with bipolar disorder or schizophrenia go untreated each year. The number of untreated people suffering from some other disorders, such as anxiety or depression, is even greater.*
- *Those most affected by the stigma include young people, men, minorities, people in the military and, perhaps surprisingly, those working in the health field.*

The American Foundation for Suicide Prevention website shares some startling statistics:

- *Every year suicide claims more lives than war, murder, and natural disasters combined, and yet suicide prevention doesn't get anywhere near the funding given to other leading causes of death.*
- *In 2013, 41,149 suicides were reported, making suicide the 10th leading cause of death for Americans...In that year, someone in the country died by suicide every 12.8 minutes.*

Please see our list of references and resources at the end of this book. Some are websites, foundations, facilities and hotlines. They are all great resources to help bring awareness of alcoholism, mental health conditions and the stigma that surrounds them.

We chose these particular pieces of information to illustrate that many people are still struggling with issues and not getting the care they need. These statistics show that millions of people struggle with mental health issues; no one is truly alone. These struggles are not character weaknesses, as many people still believe; they are valid illnesses. So why is it okay for people to suffer in silence? How can an individual break through the embarrassment they feel and get the help they need? What can our society do to create a safer environment to allow this to happen? We don't have any magic answers, just ideas to share. We want to push for more available resources and more funding in this field, including anti-stigma campaigns as indicated in the references we are providing.

Statistics from the CDC in 2010 state that *More Americans suffer from depression than coronary heart disease (17 million), cancer (12 million) and HIV/AIDS (1 million)*, so why is it so hard to tackle or even accept? The numbers don't lie. There is a gap between those who suffer and those who get help. That same fact sheet from the CDC (2010) states *90% of all people who die by suicide have a diagnosable psychiatric disorder at the time of their death, and that 105 Americans take their life each day.*

The total in 2013, as reflected in earlier statistics, was 41, 419 deaths from suicide. How can that ever be acceptable? Every one of those people had someone who loved them and will miss them. They had goals and dreams for themselves at some point in their life and lost their way. Our society must be educated to accept that mental health struggles are part of our world, and understand that it is a valid medical condition, like any other ill-ness. We cannot be afraid to talk about it, and cannot sweep these numbers under the rug of shame. They are illnesses, just like other illnesses in other parts of our bodies.

The outpouring of support since *Kevin's Story* has been incredi-bly supportive and has allowed people to open up and discuss the topics.

People want to talk about shameful issues and they seem ready, yet the barriers remain. Telling a story is a powerful and freeing process; stories can transform a person and together may trans-form our collective spirit. We hope to inspire our society to be more compassionate and accepting of whatever a person's struggle may be. This compassion may help open the door for them to get the help they need and deserve.

In closing, we want to reflect on our *7-day forecast.* The weather we have shared here started stormy and unsettled, and ended with clouds breaking for more sunshine. We hope we have shed some light on the shame that is hard to overcome and how it can weather a person. After experiencing our changeable skies, we hope our book prompts a journey of recovery to have more sunny skies ahead.

A note to our readers:

We have focused on mental health and substance abuse because that is our story. However, there are many other hard subjects to discuss, including financial struggles, illiteracy and/or lack of educational achievement, poverty, medical issues that are hidden, being adopted, sexual orientation or questioning, relationship failures and divorce, body image, domestic violence, being abused or being the abuser. These are shame issues that viewers shared with us after the airing of *Kevin's Story.*

If you have a personal story about shame and stigma, what would you want society to know about you from your perspective? Do you have ideas for how to reduce shame and stigma?

We are asking our readers to contact us either by email or in writing. We would love to hear from you. We hope to gather these thoughts and perhaps put them all together in some fashion. Give us at least your initials and a way to contact you if you are comfortable, so we can reach you for permission to use part or all in future blogs or writings. All information is confidential and would not be used without obtaining permission.

However, sending us your thoughts anonymously is fine if that is what is most comfortable for you. We truly look forward to this unique aspect of the book and our journey to spread awareness on these subjects. We also hope that providing the resources and this unique platform of collecting stories on shame and stigma will be a powerful tool.

Our email for this feedback is: *weatheringshame@yahoo.com* and our mailing address is: Weathering Shame, P.O. Box 3712,

Portland, Maine, 04104.  Even if you responded to *Kevin's Story*, which aired on WCSH and WLBZ, feel free to email or write again.  We know that with your stories and thoughts, together we will create a powerful message of hope, healing and meaningful change.

Kevin Mannix is best known as one of Maine's most popular and favorite weathermen. Serving the broadcasting world for over forty years, Mannix was part of the WCSH 6, Portland and WLBZ 2, Bangor weather team from 1989 to 2014, where he forecasted the weather for Maine and New Hampshire on the NEWS CENTER Morning Report.

Prior to joining WCSH, Mr. Mannix was a weather forecaster in Presque Isle, Phoenix, Arizona, and Worcester, Massachusetts. He graduated from Northeast Broadcasting School in Boston with a certificate in Broadcasting.

A fan favorite, Kevin has been voted Maine's favorite weatherman on several occasions and was the recipient of the 2014 Maine Association of Broadcasters for Commitment to Community Award, along with WCSH, for *Kevin's Story*. He and his wife Linda share awards for their volunteer work and have been honored by Shalom House and Crossroads Women's Center for their commitment to bring awareness on shame and stigma, beginning with the special series, *Kevin's Story*, which aired on WCSH-WBLZ TV in 2013. This series led the couple to co-author *Weathering Shame*, an autobiography on their personal experiences growing up with the stigma and shame of alcoholism and mental illness.

Kevin enjoys sports, movies, and travel. He volunteers religiously for Coats for Kids, The Waban Telethon and many other local charities. Kevin has two sons, Jeff and Taylor and resides in Portland, Maine with his wife and co-author Linda Rota.

Linda Rota, LSW, has been a social worker for over thirty years. She is a 1982 magna cum laude graduate from the University of Southern Maine where she earned a B.A. in both social welfare and criminal justice. Linda served in the Peace Corps from 1982-1984 in Sierra Leone, West Africa working as an agriculture extension agent, and assisted in the training of incoming volunteers on cross-cultural issues.

Ms. Rota's areas of social work concentration in the U.S. include child protection, substance abuse support services, mental health treatment and community integration. Over the past fifteen years, her work has focused on state and contract level child protection casework.

Linda assisted in developing and implementing three separate community integration programs, worked with grant funded projects for child abuse prevention, the intersection between substance abuse and child welfare and consumer-operated services. She has been a licensed active foster parent and has many credits towards her Masters in Public Policy and Management at the Muskie School of Public Service. A contributing author in several publications, Ms. Rota has been honored with several awards including the Children's Advocacy Council's Child Prevention Award Honoree 2008.

She enjoys spending time with her husband, family and friends, especially her two daughters and new granddaughter. Her other interests include traveling, nature, movies, music, gardening, calligraphy, camping, and relaxing by the water.

# Resources

**Websites and Organization**

*John Bradshaw Healing the Shame that Binds You*

*211.org*

*American Foundation for Suicide Prevention www.afsp.org*

*National Alliance for the Mentally Ill: www.nami.org*

*American Psychiatric Association: www.psych.org*

*Substance Abuse and Mental Health Services Administration www.samhsa.gov*

*Address Discrimination & Stigma (ADS) Center www.stop-stigma.samhsa.gov*

*National Institute of Mental Health: www.nimh.nih.gov*

*Mental Health Screening: www.mentalhealthscreening.org*

*Spring Harbor: www.springharbor.org*

*Send correspondence to:*
*Weathering Shame, PO Box 3712*
*Portland, ME 04104*
*Email: WeatheringShame@yahoo.com*

Made in the USA
Middletown, DE
30 April 2016